Confessions of a Pregnant Father

Books by Dan Greenburg

How to Be a Jewish Mother
Kiss My Firm but Pliant Lips
How to Make Yourself Miserable
Chewsday
Jumbo the Boy and Arnold the Elephant
Philly
Porno-Graphics
Scoring
Something's There
Love Kills
What Do Women Want?
How to Avoid Love and Marriage
True Adventures

Confessions of a Pregnant Father

Dan Greenburg

Macmillan Publishing Company / *New York*
Collier Macmillan Publishers / *London*

Macmillan Publishing Company
866 Third Avenue, New York, N.Y. 10022
Collier Macmillan Canada, Inc.

Library of Congress Cataloging-in-Publication Data

Greenburg, Dan.
    Confessions of a pregnant father.

    1. Greenburg, Dan.   2. Fathers—United States—
Biography.   I. Title.
HQ756.G74   1986   306.8'742   85-23199
ISBN 0-02-545450-1

10   9   8   7   6   5   4   3   2   1

Designed by Mary Cregan

Printed in the United States of America

For Suzanne and Zack with all my love

Confessions of a Pregnant Father

I HAD NEVER THOUGHT I wanted to be a father. To me babies meant all-night squalling, poopy diapers and sticky fingerprints on everything you owned. Babies also meant terrible restrictions on one's time and mobility. I had always resented any restrictions on my time and mobility. I had always led an extremely self-indulgent life.

Whenever my friends became fathers, I had marveled at and pitied their willingness to inflict upon themselves the all-night squalling, poopy diapers, sticky fingerprints, and restriction of time and mobility that came with fatherhood.

Needless to say, the above-named inconveniences were not the most important reasons I had opted out of fatherhood. There were also the fears.

Fear of producing a physically or mentally impaired baby and having that poison my life forever. Fear that having a child would automatically place me on the conveyor belt that carries one relentlessly from fatherhood to grandfatherhood to the grave. Fear that I might finally be forced to grow up.

I had the notion that fatherhood just wasn't something I wanted to do this time around. There was some fuzzy feeling that it might be more appealing, oh, *next* time, although I can't tell you what that means, since I don't believe in reincarnation.

Despite my fears of fatherhood, I had strong nurturing urges. These I sublimated for years with a succession of pussycats upon whom I doted to a sometimes embarrassing degree.

My first wife was similarly ambivalent about children during the seven or so years we were together, and she doted equally upon our cats.

Three years after my divorce I met Suzanne O'Malley, an Irish-Catholic beauty from Dallas, Texas, and a senior editor at *Esquire* magazine. I was 40, Suzanne was 25. She made it clear to me on our second date that she wished someday to be married and have children. In what must have been a terribly appealing speech, I told her I had not the slightest desire to have children, to get married again, or to live with another human being. Suzanne figured I was protesting too much, and opted to stick around and help me change my mind.

Our courtship deepened into a quite romantic love, although not at breakneck speed. Two years after we met I asked her to move into my apartment. Two years after that I bought her an armload of pink roses, took her for drinks at The Four Seasons and then to dinner at the Rainbow Room atop the RCA Building, swept her out onto the dance floor, and popped the question.

"I have something to ask you," I said.

"*Yes*," she said.

"Will you marry me?" I said.

"*Yes*, I already said *yes*," she replied, and turned to a short elderly couple dancing next to us. "This man has just asked me to marry him," she announced.

"Mazel tov," said the man.

"Tell him you'll think about it," said the woman.

We had a big romantic wedding at the Lotos Club in New York. Four years after that, in my forty-seventh year, we decided we were ready to have a child.

Yes, I still had my fears, but I was willing to deal with them.

I had gotten to the point in therapy and in life that dodging my fears was even less comfortable than confronting them.

Irresponsible fun was no longer such a novelty. I had been living self-indulgently for many years, the champagne had already gone a bit flat, and the prospect of continuing in the same vein for the rest of my life was distasteful to me. I was ready to seek more in this world than my own selfish desires. My self-image had changed. After years as a loner and a rebel, I found myself longing for membership and legitimacy.

Suzanne, who had chosen me despite my widely advertised disinterest in paternity and had all but resigned herself to childlessness, still wanted to be a mother. I had come to the surprising realizations that I was unwilling to miss the experience of fathering a child after all, that there wasn't going to be a next time, and that I was on that conveyor belt to the grave whether I became a father or not.

✳

Perhaps there yet exists a place where, having decided to procreate, the next thing that a man and woman do is go straight to bed and have sex. Among urban middle-class New York couples like us, the next thing that a man and woman do is to go to a real estate broker and try to buy a larger apartment than they can afford.

We had been living in the upper half of a small brownstone in midtown Manhattan. A bedroom, an office, and two baths on the entry floor. A kitchen, a dining room, a half bath, and a living room with a double-height ceiling on the next floor. And an enclosed greenhouse on the top floor. It was marvelous for anything but children. There were no bedrooms but ours.

We put our apartment on the market and registered with half a dozen real estate brokers. We spent the better part of a year running around New York, looking at terminally boring but outrageously overpriced three-bedroom apartments with surreal monthly carrying charges, fighting about places that one of us liked and the other loathed. We saw nothing that both of us could agree upon unless it cost as much as Blenheim Palace.

During this period we were also doing a lot of travelling. We had written a humorous book together about relationships called *How to Avoid Love and Marriage*, and we were spending the better part of four months doing publicity for it in this country's top forty cities.

Almost every day during this four-month stretch we awoke at 5:30 A.M. in a new hotel in a new city and went off to do eight or ten interviews on TV and radio and in the press. At the end of the day we flew on to the next city on our schedule and began the process all over again. It was exciting and fun for the first couple of weeks, but after that it was only exhausting. Suzanne had the flu and I fought off two viruses. We both averaged four hours sleep per night.

Every so often we returned to New York for a few days and spent the entire time racing around to inspect co-op apartments. We were soon familiar with every three-bedroom apartment in New York and we still found nothing we liked.

The real estate brokers got as bored with us as we got with them, and this was no mean feat. We realized it was stupid to keep looking for an apartment to buy until we had a buyer for our own apartment, and we had nothing of the kind.

Oh, a few couples had meandered desultorily through our apartment and muttered vaguely demeaning things about it, but nobody lingered to make even a half-serious offer. I grew increasingly testy toward real estate agents and prospective buyers, taking each rejection in only the most personal and emotional terms.

Finally a nice, solvent couple came along, loved our apartment, and agreed to our asking price. We made a verbal deal, left for another week of publicity, and then, in a hotel in Philadelphia, we panicked. Up to now Suzanne had been dying to get rid of this apartment in which I had lived with a previous wife, an apartment in which I'd had illicit carnal relations with other women during the four years between marriages. Now she was in tears at the notion of actually giving it up, particularly since we'd found no place else to move.

We called the nice, solvent couple with whom we had made a deal in good faith, and we told them that we would only sell them our apartment if we could find something as good as ours for the same price. The nice and solvent couple was quite understandably pissed.

Upon our return to New York the search for places to move was no more successful with a buyer for our apartment than it had been without one. Eventually the nice, solvent couple got legitimately fed up with us and bought somebody else's apartment. There was nothing left to do but renovate.

*

Renovation is, I am told, high up on the list of Most Stressful Life Experiences, somewhere between Messy Divorce and The Loss of Both Arms and Legs. The pain of renovation, as Suzanne has recently observed, must be as hard to recall as the pain of childbirth, or else why would people have two, three, even four renovations?

Our apartment is in the upper three floors of a small building that used to be the parish house of an Episcopal church. An interior designer had gutted the building and renovated it from the ground up in 1964. He lived in what is now our apartment himself until 1970, whereupon he sold it to me for a nice profit and moved his practice out of the city.

Our house in East Hampton, Long Island, is in the woods about five minutes' drive from the Atlantic Ocean. It has three bedrooms, a long living-dining room, a large kitchen, and every room has a sliding glass door which opens to the outside. The East Hampton house is now as contemporary and geometric as is our city apartment, and the massive renovation we did to make it that way was virtually painless. There was absolutely no reason to suspect that the renovation of our city apartment would be any more difficult.

We first met with our newly chosen and highly recommended designer, one Percy Duckworth, in February 1984. We discussed our decision to make what was then our office into a baby and nanny's room, to change what was then the greenhouse into our office. We also wanted some closets relocated, a washer-dryer installed, the kitchen and downstairs bathrooms enlarged and updated, and so on.

Percy made some sketches, we met with his contractor, and we set up a schedule: Percy would give us finished working drawings no later than March 1, whereupon he would apply for a building permit. A building permit, Percy said, took three months to get in New York, so we would begin the actual construction when it arrived, on June 1. We would pack up everything we owned and move to East Hampton on June 1. The construction would take four months, and we would move back to New York on October 1. The contractor and Percy assured us it was a viable plan, and we believed them.

Those readers who have had direct personal experience with renovations are by now rolling on the floor, helpless with mirth, perhaps even devising ways to sell us speculative real estate in the Everglades, but our previous renovation had gone so smoothly that we allowed ourselves to believe his schedule.

*

February 29, 1984. We were exhausted from publicity tours and apartment hunting. We decided to take a relaxing vacation and to begin building this baby we were renovating an apartment around.

In view of the impending renovation, we did not have a lot of money to spend on a relaxing vacation. Fortunately, however, we had been kicked off an overbooked Republic Airlines flight from Traverse City, Michigan, to New York City the previous summer and were given two free round-trip tickets to anywhere Republic flew. The farthest away that Republic flew was Grand Cayman Island in the Caribbean.

Our travel agent hadn't been to Grand Cayman Island, but her reference books described it glowingly. They recommended in particular a hotel called the Terrapin Club, which sounded small and informal and just what the obstetrician ordered. We booked a bungalow on the beach for ten days and flew down to Grand Cayman.

*

After a queasy approach and a boneshakingly hard landing at the Grand Cayman airport, we emerge from the tiny terminal. The weather is not the steamy, fragrant, tropical night one expects in the Caribbean. It is windy, rainy, and rather chilly.

We look around for the hotel bus that is supposed to meet us, but do not see it. A muscular native woman in masculine attire approaches us and says she has been sent to take us back to the Terrapin Club. We get into her beat-up mini-car for the hour-long drive to the hotel.

To make polite small talk with our drive on the lengthy trip, we ask how the weather has been.

"Today ees de feeft day of de storm," says our driver matter-of-factly.

"The fifth day of the storm," I say. "I see. And, uh, how long is this storm expected to last?"

"Maybe two day, maybe tree day," she says defensively, "nobody can know thees."

"I see," I say.

"Is the hotel busy?" says Suzanne.

"Beesy? No no," says our driver. "There ees only one more couple at de hotel now, and dey leaving tomorrow."

It's true we had hoped for a quiet place in which to relax and mate. Having the entire hotel to ourselves wasn't really necessary.

"Tell me," I say, "is the Terrapin Club as lovely as the guidebooks have described it?"

"De Terrapin Club," says our driver, "ees once de showplace of de Cayman Islands."

"Once?" I say.

"Den de first owner he sell de Club, and de new owner he let de place run down very bod, and now de Terrapin Club ees een receiversheep."

Not willing to dwell too long upon the concept of being stuck on a faraway Caribbean island in a hotel that is in receivership, we ask if, at least, the beach is pretty.

"Oh yes," says our driver, "de beach ees very pretty. Ond dere ees notheeng to worry about."

"Uh, what is there not to worry about?" I ask, not having imagined that there was anything to worry about.

"Hostile natives on de beach," she says. "De natives dey not at all hostile."

I choose to dismiss this ominously gratuitous reassurance and focus instead upon our long-standing desire to learn how to sail. We ask if the hotel has sailboats, as we had been told.

"Oh yes," says our driver, "de hotel hov two sailboats, but you must sail dem een exactly de direction dat we tell you, or else ees very dangerous."

"Why is that?" I ask, aware that I am in some kind of living Bob Newhart routine.

"Well," she says, "one guest he sail een de wrong direction, he capsize de boat on de coral reef wheech ees covered weeth de sea urchins, ond he stung so bod dey hov to take heem to de hospital."

"Did he survive?" asks Suzanne.

"Oh yes, he survive," says our driver. "But dere ees not too much he can do when he get out of de hospital, so he go home."

For the duration of the journey we will both silently ponder the sea-urchin-stung man who could not do too much when he got out of the hospital.

We arrive at the hotel in total darkness, and it is impossible to see enough to tell whether we are moving into paradise or purgatory. Our driver carries our bags into a room with cinderblock walls, which is lit by a snapping fluorescent tube that looks like a cheap strobe in a fifth-rate disco.

We assume that this is the baggage room. We are wrong. It is not the baggage room. It is *our* room.

In the light of the snapping fluorescent tube we can see that the furniture is shabby, that the bedspread is full of holes and cigarette burns, and that the bed itself sags so badly it looks more like a place to bathe than a place to sleep. In lieu of a clothes closet there is a corroded horizontal bar hung adjacent to the front door, from which are suspended six grotesquely twisted wire hangers.

We go into the bathroom to find a sputtering shower that has water which is either scalding or freezing, but nothing in between, a toilet that takes twenty minutes to flush, leaking faucets that have rusted and been painted over and rusted through the paint, and a medicine cabinet that hasn't been cleaned in twelve years.

It is hardly the romantic little Caribbean hideaway we thought we'd chosen to conceive our baby. It is, of course, too late to do anything about it tonight, but we will see about better accommodations in the morning.

In the morning we awake to frightening winds and horizontal rain, and the sound of the only other couple in the hotel having an ugly marital squabble in the room next to ours.

We try to find other hotels in which to stay but they are all booked solid, even the Holiday Inn. When we tell the other hotels that we are at the Terrapin Club, they cluck their tongues and express condolences.

We are too exhausted to spend an entire day on the hotel's only phone, calling up other islands and trying to get accommodations on such short notice. We cannot bear the idea of flying right back to New York. We decide to remain at the Terrapin Club. It is like a bad play by Sartre.

The food at the Terrapin Club, is for some unknown reason, surprisingly decent, but at dinner Suzanne observes a large furry brown rodent running across the rush matting on the wall just over our heads.

"A rat!" Suzanne screams, irritating the staff.

That night, while we sleep, another rat (OK, maybe the *same* rat) eats through a bag of cookies on our dresser, and chews through a Baggie I have brought which is filled with mixed vitamins—if this rat also does aerobic exercise three times a week like I do, he is one healthy son of a bitch.

There are immense roaches in our bathroom. The swimming beach is strewn with slag, tar, and refuse. The shallow water nearest the beach is crowded with sharp rocks, beds of poisonous sea urchins, and semi-poisonous sea grasses.

By the third day the storm has blown out to sea, and a hot sun emerges. We lie outside on the scruffy sand and bake our pale skins. We have become used to the hotel, the rats, the roaches, and the sea urchins. We've befriended a recently arrived couple in the way that you befriend people in the army, and we've decided to make the best of things and have a good time. We rent a car and go sightseeing.

Grand Cayman Island is flat, the vegetation sparse, the beaches narrow and rocky. We are told that Cayman Islanders have the highest standard of living of any Caribbean island. Indeed, we notice a gigantic TV satellite dish parked outside almost every other native's house. A satellite dish happens to be one of the only two ways that Cayman Islanders can watch television. The other way is that videocassettes of all popular American TV shows, including news programs, are flown into the island every few days. Most natives on this island, we are told, own videocassette recorders—how hostile could they be?

The Cayman Islands are known for sea turtles, scuba diving, and banking. There are 500 banks in Georgetown, the place where we landed, and that is a lot of banks for a small Caribbean town. It would even be a lot of banks for Detroit. Reportedly, a good deal of international money is laundered here. "We come here for the banking," I become fond of saying. The quip wears thin after a few days.

We make love every day—the tropical setting is not entirely unromantic, and there is almost nothing else to do. We feel certain we are going to be immediately successful at making a baby.

The daytime sun is scorching, and we soon develop attractive and painful tans. The water is nice to swim in, provided that you can find a way to get into it without walking through the shallow part in bare feet. We learn to walk through the shallow part in swim fins. We are having a pretty good time.

We don't even get too upset when our toilet stops flushing altogether and we have to use the one in the unoccupied room next door, or when the hotel's fresh water supply runs out and there is no water at all that day, or when a rat eats an entire roll of toilet paper in our bathroom one night.

A few days before we are to leave, a maid who is cleaning our room says to us with no provocation whatsoever: "Thees place ees not feet to leev en—are you not ongry dey chargeeng you so much money to stay here?"

On our final night we hold a drunken farewell banquet with the two couples we have gotten to know, as a new tropical storm hurls itself against the dining room and threatens to shatter the windows.

*

Within a few weeks of our return to New York, we realize that the purpose of the trip to Grand Cayman has not been fulfilled—Suzanne's period has arrived right on schedule.

Not only does she fail to conceive in March, she doesn't conceive in April either. It is becoming clear that making a baby is not simply a matter of throwing away one's diaphragm. It is ludicrous that we have spent so much effort in previous years trying *not* to conceive—if we had only known how hard it was. Each of us is privately certain that the other is the problem.

Suzanne's obstetrician learns of our baby-making attempts and warns darkly that if we are unable to conceive within twelve months we classify as an infertility case. Three couples we know confide that they were infertility cases. All three husbands and wives were examined. All three husbands were diagnosed as having low sperm counts. All three husbands went into various hospitals and had varicocelectomies.

A varicocelectomy is a minor operation on your testicles to remove a varicose vein. I cannot even *begin* to tell you how disinterested I am in going anywhere and having anybody do anything to my testicles with a sharp instrument.

We decide to apply as much thought to conception as we did in the past to contraception. We learn that one way to help the sperm get to the womb is for the woman to remain in bed with her legs elevated for thirty to sixty minutes after intercourse, so every time we make love Suzanne remains in bed with her legs raised for almost an hour.

A woman's temperature dips lowest just before she ovulates. So if the idea is to make a baby, the best time to impregnate is when a woman's temperature is the lowest. This means Suzanne cannot discover her lowest temperature unless she takes it every day—at the moment of waking, when it is lower than any point in the day—and unless she keeps precise daily records of those waking temperatures, at the same time every morning, for at least a couple of months.

We buy an Ovulindex thermometer, which only registers temperatures between 96 and 100 degrees Fahrenheit, and which divides each degree into ten clear increments for easy reading.

We make up a chart with the days of the month. I set the

alarm clock for the same hour every morning, wake up and take Suzanne's temperature, and note it on the chart. Every morning on which we discover a low thermometer reading we make love *immediately* after temperature-taking. One morning we make love *during* temperature-taking. It is, frankly, not the most efficient way to get an accurate reading.

We try to make love every morning during fertile periods, even if we are still asleep, even if we aren't in the mood, even if we have a headache, even if we have had a fight the night before and are still smoldering.

*

Percy Duckworth's working drawings have not appeared on March 1 or April 1 or even May 1, but he assures us that he has applied for the building permit and that it will definitely arrive by July 1.

On July 1, having piled all our furniture, office equipment, books, manuscripts, winter clothing, and so on in the middle of the living room floor and thrown a dropcloth over them, we move out to East Hampton. We continue to have inconclusive meetings with Percy Duckworth. Percy Duckworth is like a naughty student who has not done his homework. There are many excuses, a lot of covering up, and no working drawings.

The building permit is arriving any day now, Percy tells us. The contractor and his crew are poised to begin work the instant the permit comes. In the meantime, Percy has hired an architect named Seymour Bung, who is licensed in New York as Percy is not, to do a few technical drawings and sign the blueprints.

*

Our perseverance with temperature-taking and chart notations and raised legs finally pays off—at the end of July we learn by phone from the gynecologist's office that Suzanne is pregnant! We are ecstatic at the news, hug each other, and dance around the house with joy. The baby will arrive on St. Patrick's Day, March 17. We call the family and a few close friends.

George Ramsay is my former college roommate, who got married immediately after graduation and who now has a married daughter and a son in college. "Well, Greenburg," he tells me, "you always *did* do everything backwards." Quips a friend named Jim Kirkwood upon being told that Suzanne is pregnant: "Is the baby Dan's?"

Everyone who has kids welcomes us to the fraternity with the same remark: "Your life will never be the same." This statement gives me the willies, because I rather liked my life before. Suzanne wonders aloud if what they're saying isn't a trifle hostile: You had such a carefree single existence before, while we were miserable raising children—now you'll have to suffer like the rest of us.

My younger sister Naomi, who has two rambunctious sons, removes all doubt about what they are telling us. "Your life will never be the same," she says gleefully. "It will be living hell. We never got more than two hours' sleep a night for the first two years."

My mother is delighted at our news, and asks Suzanne about her "gynie-man." Her *gynie-man?* Where did my seventy-seven-year-old Jewish mother get this appellation for gynecologists, from a Calypso song? ("Come, mistah gynie-man, tolly me ba-nan-na . . .")

I buy a book entitled *The First Nine Months of Life*, which has remarkable photographs of fetuses from conception to delivery. The fetuses, in the first several months, look more like extraterrestrials in science fiction movies than human babies, but I find out some fairly astounding facts.

For example, did you know that the human embryo expands 10,000 times in size within the first thirty days? Or that when the embryo is only forty days old it's so small it weighs less than a book of paper matches and would fit into a walnut shell with room to spare. Yet it has a brain, a nervous system, and a heart that has been beating for two weeks.

A few days after hearing and telling the news of the pregnancy, a great sense of anticlimax overtakes us. Our lives have not changed. No baby has suddenly popped out from under a cabbage plant. Suzanne's belly has not grown. Everything is just as it was before we knew that she was pregnant. The joy and the reality of the pregnancy begin to slip away from us. We no longer feel like making love—it's as if procreation had somehow been our primary goal in sex.

*

The working drawings and the building permit, of course, do not appear in July, and on August 1 Percy Duckworth goes on a month-long cruise to France on the *Q.E.2*. Seymour Bung disappears into the wilds of Fire Island and is never seen by any living human again. After leaving countless phone messages on Bung's answering machine with no response, we fire him by telegram. He sends back a charming letter saying he wouldn't have wanted to work for us anyway.

We hire another architect, James McCullar by name, to complete the drawings that neither Percy Duckworth nor Seymour Bung had done. We also find out, to our utter consternation, that the building permit which Percy Duckworth *swore* he'd applied for back in March has never been applied for at all! We have lost at least five valuable months.

*

Pregnant women are said to develop irresistible urges to wolf down exotic foods like banana splits and sushi. Suzanne points out that she has *always* had irresistible urges to wolf down exotic foods like banana splits and sushi, so pregnancy has produced no marked change in her cravings. There is no morning sickness. There is, after awhile, evening sickness. Suzanne finds herself nauseated several evenings a week and unable to eat dinner. Other than that, there is no further evidence that she is growing a fetus.

I begin to manifest sympathetic symptoms. I am frequently nauseous during the late afternoon and evening. I begin to put on extra weight around my normally flat belly.

I notice my reaction to small children is changing. Irritation at their very presence shifts inexplicably into fond amusement at even their less attractive shenanigans. I begin to chuckle at strangers' toddlers in public and find myself nudging Suzanne, even when the toddlers in question are less than comely. I have come full circle on children and I'm not even a father yet.

*

How to Avoid Love and Marriage, our tongue-in-cheek instruction manual on how to destroy deep personal relationships, is about to be published in England. We have been invited to go to London for a week in mid-September to do publicity. We figure Suzanne will finish her first trimester by then and phase out of her evening sickness. We conclude this maybe our last chance to travel for a long while to come, so we make plans to go to Ireland for a few days after England, and to Paris for a few days after that.

Suzanne has never been to Ireland, and has always wanted to look up her ancestors in County Limerick. We love Paris, and I even have two legitimate business reasons to go there now—a French play based on my book *How to Be a Jewish Mother* has been a huge hit on the Paris stage for the past year, and a French edition of another of my books, *How to Make Yourself Miserable*, is about to be published there.

Suzanne points out that the French also make the best baby clothes, and the exchange rate is so favorable to U.S. dollars that we can buy an entire baby wardrobe for about half what it would cost here.

*

Suzanne is not the only woman to be conspicuously pregnant during this period. Famous pregnancies concurrent with Suzanne's are Christina Onassis, Lucie Arnaz, Farrah Fawcett, Pia Zadora, and Ling-Ling the Panda.

*

Suzanne has bought a new book, *The Pregnancy Book for Today's Woman*, by Howard I. Shapiro, M.D. One of my biggest fears about pregnancy is that our three cats might infect Suzanne with a disease called toxoplasmosis which, I have heard, could be dangerous to pregnant women.

I am fairly sure my fears are greatly exaggerated. I look up toxoplasmosis in the book, hoping to be reassured. On p. 272 I read:

Does a cat present risks to the pregnant woman?

Yes. Of all diseases caused by household pets, none has aroused more attention and concern among pregnant women than toxoplasmosis. This disease, caused by a microscopic protozoan named *Toxoplasma gondii*, is commonly transmitted by contact with infected cat feces or by the handling or eating of infected raw meat. Adults who contract the disease usually have no symptoms and never know they have it . . .

If a woman contracts toxoplasmosis during the first trimester of pregnancy, it is estimated that her fetus will have a 17 percent risk of becoming infected. Of this 17 percent, 80 percent will be stillborn or show severe manifestations of the disease such as microcephaly (abnormally small head), hydrocephaly (abnormally large head), cerebral calcifications, blindness due to destruction of the retina, and convulsions. . . .

The day we found out Suzanne was pregnant, she stopped changing the cat litter. We also stopped allowing our cats, Gladys, Wendell, and Maurice, to sleep with us in our bed at night, and we no longer permitted them to go outside.

The cats were outraged at the inexplicable curtailment of their outdoor privileges. One day Wendell was standing at the sliding screen door, gazing wistfully at the wildlife with his front paws on the screen. His claws got caught in the screen, and, in the process of disengaging them, he accidentally yanked the screen partially open. Gladys, who is much smarter than Wendell, observed what he had done and then figured out how to open the screen door. (This is how we humans learned to make fire, cook meat, and pre-program videocassette recorders.) Anytime Gladys likes now, she can slide the screen open and let herself, Wendell, and Maurice outside.

From this point on, we keep the sliding glass door as well as the sliding screen door closed, even in hot weather. Since our house has eight sliding glass doors and no windows, it's uncomfortable on really warm days, but we feel it is worth it.

Then Gladys figures out that glass sliders work the same as screen sliders, and succeeds in getting these open as well. She and Wendell manage to spend a few madcap hours in the woods adjoining our house before we can recapture them. We will now have to keep the sliders not only closed but locked.

Terribly nervous about the cats' recent woodland jaunt, I call our East Hampton vet and ask whether there is a test for toxoplasmosis. He says there is—if I like I can bring in the cats' feces to be analyzed in the lab. I sift through the litter box and collect their turds in little empty Dannon yogurt containers and schlepp them off to the vet.

In the meantime Suzanne is tested at the obstetrician for toxoplasmosis. If she's been exposed to it before, there will be antibodies in her blood and she is safe. The test comes back negative—she does not have toxoplasmosis, but there are also no antibodies present. Suzanne is not safe, and could become infected if exposed to the toxoplasmosis virus.

The cats' turds are analyzed and no toxoplasmosis virus is found, but the vet admits this is no assurance the cats aren't carriers. There is another test, he tells us, which involves drawing blood tests from the cats on two occasions, three weeks apart. If there is a significant rise in the level of antibodies in their blood from one test to the other, then they are "hot" and need to be given away till the baby is born.

We take the cats for their blood tests and wait nervously for the three weeks between tests and the additional few days to get the results.

The tests show that all three cats have been exposed to toxoplasmosis in the past, but there is no significant rise in their antibody levels, so they are not "hot." We breathe a tremendous sigh of relief and continue to keep the sliding doors closed and locked.

Before we leave for Europe we invite two dear friends, Lee Frank and Jan Weil, to East Hampton for one of the weekends we'll be gone. We impress upon them the need to keep the cats inside and the sliders closed and locked. We ask them to leave their own cats in New York so as not to run the risk of passing toxoplasmosis on to ours if their cats are carriers.

*

September 15. We fly to England and spend a week publicizing *How to Avoid Love and Marriage*. As it is on American publicity tours, we find ourselves getting up at 5:30 A.M. and spending the day running all over the place doing interviews. As it is not on American publicity tours, the interviewers in England all appear to understand the tongue-in-cheek humor of the book and don't have to begin each interview by asking, "Why would we want to learn how to *avoid* love and marriage?"

We do radio interviews in London, Brighton, Birmingham, Coventry, and Oxford, and once more average four hours of sleep per night. I am worried about the effect of so much exhausting activity on Suzanne's pregnancy, but she appears to be holding up fine. Suzanne has a few periods of evening sickness, but our interviews are never in the evening.

On September 22 we leave England and fly to Ireland. We rent a tiny Fiat with right-hand steering and spend four days driving through the Irish countryside, searching for O'Malleys in the baptismal records of ancient Catholic churches and graveyards and in the homes of ancient Irish priests. Our first night we stay in a fifteenth-century castle which is closed for the season, but which Suzanne has persuaded its owners to reopen for us.

The castle owners are, I discover, intensely interested in the occult. The castle is spooky, and unheated. We are so cold at night we have to sleep with all our clothes on. In the morning we move to a regular hotel, but the experience has inspired me to begin writing a Gothic horror novel.

We find nothing conclusive regarding Suzanne's roots in County Limerick, and on September 26 we fly to Paris. In the marvelous department store Au Printemps, Suzanne buys Clarins oil to rub on her belly to prevent stretchmarks, and we shop for baby clothes. Any baby clothes with flop-eared bunnies on them reduce me to a gibbering idiot. We end up buying lots of baby clothes featuring flop-eared bunnies.

*

September 30. Upon our return to East Hampton we learn that Lee and Jan misunderstood our warnings about toxoplasmosis and brought their cats to our house for the weekend. Further, they didn't realize that Gladys could actually open a closed sliding glass door, and they failed to lock the one in the kitchen. Gladys opened it and all three cats spent a rambunctious night in the woods. Lee and Jan realized what they'd done and panicked. They spent half the night in the woods, trying to get the cats to come back, in the course of which Jan slipped and broke her leg.

We are quite upset with Lee and Jan. We no longer feel that the cats are safe. Our morbid fears about birth defects return. I go back to the vet and ask if he can do more blood tests. He assures me there are no further tests to be done and no further assurances to be had. In his opinion, the cats are probably safe.

I go through several days of fantasizing horrid things—a baby born with a grotesquely tiny head, a baby born with a grotesquely large head, a life filled with misery. I torture myself about whether I would have the courage to raise a deformed child or whether I would send it to an institution.

Finally, the years I have spent in therapy allow me to regain my senses. I realize there is nothing more to be done—when the baby comes, and only then, will we find out whether it has been damaged by toxoplasmosis, or by something else. I realize that I can either spend the rest of the pregnancy torturing myself, or I can let go of my fears and enjoy the pregnancy—for the same money I can spend the time feeling good instead of bad.

I decide to feel good, and the fears slip away. It's as simple as that. Amazing.

*

Although we had been scheduled to move back into our New York apartment on October 1, that is the day construction actually begins. I say construction, but it is actually demolition. By mid-October, every room in our apartment has been demolished. Huge poles are gouged out of walls and floors and ceilings. Pipes and wires hang free, and a thick layer of plaster dust covers everything.

In past years, every Labor Day we had flirted with the notion of not going back to New York and staying in East Hampton through winter. Every year we watched the summer people leave, we breathed a sigh of relief, and then it got *very* quiet. Most of the summer stores and restaurants closed up until spring, and the cold winds began to whine through the naked trees.

Every October we packed up and went back to the city. Every October but this one. This year, thanks to Percy Duckworth, we don't have that choice. I have always been a city boy, first in Chicago, then in Los Angeles, then in New York. Living out in the country through the winter will be an adventure. The Häagen-Dazs store closes for the season and we buy ice cream for half price, wondering if this is hearty winter food.

We realize that we will soon need a larger and more practical car than our old 1964 Porsche to cart around baby paraphernalia, and so we buy a Jeep Cherokee with four-wheel drive so we can also drive through the winter snows.

It is not that we are going to be completely isolated from civilization like the Donner party. Our house is in the woods, but we do have heat and light and cable TV. And we do have to go into the city almost every week to supervise the renovation, to go to the obstetrician, to go to our various shrinks, and, starting in late January, to go to Lamaze classes. We have been assured by our contractor that we will *definitely* be able to live in our apartment by late January, if not before, no *problem.*

The contractor gives us the official estimates from all the trades for the renovation. The estimates are, needless to say, substantially higher than we had anticipated. They will be higher yet, because Percy Duckworth never included little details like electric lights and wall outlets and heating units and air-conditioning and ducting on his sketchy working drawings, and so all of these will be extra, and charged at higher, noncompetitive rates.

At first we go into New York on Tuesday afternoons and come back on Thursdays, and stay at the apartments of friends. The Jeep is about eighty times more comfortable on the highway than our elderly Porsche, and as the weather gets frigid, we are grateful that we are not driving a convertible without a heater.

Staying at the apartments of friends begins to lose its thrill after several weeks, for us as well as for our friends. We switch to driving into the city just for the day and coming back late in the evening. When we drive back at night, we establish a tradition of stopping at a diner on the state route that connects the Long Island Expressway with the Sunrise Highway, and we order pancakes and eggs.

The feeling between us on our late night drives back to East Hampton and in the diner over our pancakes and eggs is extremely warm and intimate, and these moments become very special to us—our pregnancy is a shared adventure which draws us together as it shuts out everybody else.

The fetus has expanded into most of the space Suzanne was using to keep her bladder, making it no longer possible for her to last an entire trip on the Long Island Expressway without urinating. Since there are no service stations on the expressway itself, Suzanne has me regularly pull onto the shoulder of the highway so she can pee off the side of the car, while I watch to see that nobody is coming.

I can only watch, of course; I cannot prevent. Many people who drive the Long Island Expressway in the autumn of 1984 catch fleeting glimpses of Suzanne peeing off the side of our jeep.

Suzanne's belly has not grown as much as she'd expected it would by this time, and she is self-conscious about not showing enough, but her breasts are expanding at an alarming rate. She has gone from a bra size of 34C to 36C to 36D to 36DD to 36DD with a bra extender. It is as if somebody is steadily blowing her breasts full of air like beachballs. I worry that they will explode.

One day I walk into our bathroom and come face-to-face with Suzanne's latest brassiere. It is enormous. It is draped casually over the shower door. There is something ominous about this brassiere. It is too big. It is somehow . . . unnatural. It has . . . a life of its own. It does not please me to admit this, but I am not comfortable being alone with this brassiere. Watching it carefully for the slightest hint of something malevolent, I back slowly out of the bathroom.

*

October 22. We haven't been sure before but today we are—the baby is definitely kicking. I can put my hand on Suzanne's belly and feel a number of strong and erratically timed kicks. At times I don't even have to put my hand there—I can see something within poking the skin of her belly out.

It's exciting, of course, but it is a rather peculiar phenomenon, to say the least, the notion that something alive—something not you—is inside your gut. Shades of *Alien*. Mel Brooks, in his "2,000-Year-Old Man" album, explains why pregnant women are nauseated so much: "The first time you realize there's something *alive* in there . . . you *puke*."

*

November 14. We have decided to get a sonogram. Using sound waves that bounce off the fetus, a sonogram projects an image of the fetus onto a video monitor. From this image doctors can tell a lot about the normalcy of the fetus. They can also tell what sex it is, but you are not supposed to get a sonogram if all you want to know is your baby's sex—a sonogram, we are told repeatedly, is not a toy.

Suzanne lies down on an examination table in the sonogram doctor's office, and a female technician moves what looks like a flashlight attached to an electrical cord over Suzanne's belly. The sonogram appears on a video monitor which resembles a very small black-and-white television.

We look in awe at the screen. We have absolutely no idea what we are looking at. The technician points out the fetus's head, buttocks, arms, and legs, and after awhile we can pretty much identify the various parts ourselves.

"There's the head!" I say excitedly.

"Well, uh, no, that's the buttocks," says the technician.

I have brought three cameras and take many more pictures than anybody needs of a very small black-and-white television set with the sort of reception you might get if you replaced your cable hookup with a wire coat hanger. We realize we are looking at our actual baby for the first time. It is an emotional moment.

The fetus is in constant motion on the TV screen—turning, wriggling, doing slow somersaults, moving around just the way Suzanne had imagined it was doing in her belly. At one point the fetus scratches its head, as if in embryonic puzzlement. At another it casually crosses its legs at the ankle, as you or I might do while resting them on an ottoman or a coffee table. We are knocked out by our kid's antics.

"Would you like to know what sex it is?" says the technician almost off-handedly.

We have been told so many times that a sonogram is not a toy, that it is to be used only if there is some question about fetal health and *not* to satisfy parents' curiosity about their baby's sex, that we feel a little guilty even replying to this question.

We exchange a silent glance.

"Yes," we say in unison.

"It's a boy," says the technician.

So there it is. Like most of the important moments in my life, this one just sneaked right up on me without fanfare and before I had a chance to prepare myself.

Assuming that the technician is correct—gender identification from sonograms is only 75 percent accurate—this casually offered piece of information will affect our lives in more ways than I am right now willing to contemplate.

"How can you tell it's a boy?"

"Look right here," says the technician, pointing to a small dark shape between the fetus's legs. "There's his penis. It's quite a good-sized one, too, by the way."

I have a curious reaction looking at the tiny dark shape which the technician has identified as my son's penis. I find I am uncomfortable with it. I find it vaguely threatening to be told that I have a son with a large penis. How could I possibly feel threatened by a fetus penis? Am I in sexual competition with an embryo or what?

Of course I am delighted to know it's a boy. I would have been equally delighted to know it was a girl. If it had been a girl, she would always have loved me, even if she one day grew alienated from Suzanne. If it really is a boy, I know there must come a time when he will choose to act as though he no longer loves me—when he will have to separate himself from me if he is to become his own man, as I had to separate myself from my own father. It is a saddening, if wholly premature, thought.

We had been thinking about naming the baby Dallas if it were a girl (in honor of Suzanne's hometown), Zack if it were a boy (no reason except that we liked the name). We begin calling the fetus Zack.

*

November 15. The following afternoon in my therapy group, I tell of the sonogram, of the news that the baby is probably a boy, and of the size of his probable penis.

Two of the women in the group misunderstand what I have told them and become instant feminist parodies, accusing me of swaggering macho pride at having a son with a large penis. I am exasperated and hurt at having been so ironically misunderstood and I say so.

*

The progress on the construction in our New York apartment has not been staggering. It looks much the way it did a month or two ago, except it is now so filthy that the workmen have lost respect for it and begun to abuse it. There are squashed beer cans and coffee cups and cigarettes all over the place. There are graffiti on the walls and on Suzanne's desk where the phone is, and even on the phone itself. Attempts to urinate in the toilet rather than on the floor have been largely abandoned. It makes me sick to go there.

In order to keep our sanity, we make a decision to dissociate ourselves from the apartment emotionally. We stop referring to it as our apartment. We start calling it what the workmen call it—the jobsite.

*

Around Thanksgiving, in her fifth month, Suzanne begins to "show." That is, her belly is now big enough for people to see that she is pregnant. Suzanne is relieved, having complained for months that she had no evidence she was really pregnant. I am proud, yet also strangely self-conscious, even embarrassed, as if her belly is proof that we have been doing something naughty.

We hold a family Thanksgiving dinner in East Hampton and invite my mother from Chicago, my cousins from New York, Mathew and Sheila Intner and their grown children Susan, Jonathan, Carol, and Carol's husband, Eric Henry. Eric is 28, Carol, 29, and they are expecting a baby about twelve days after we are, although Carol is showing more than Suzanne.

Eric and I swap expectant dad anxieties, and the fact that I am old enough to be *his* father does not entirely escape me.

*

January 4, 1985. We are in our seventh month of pregnancy. At 8:00 this evening we join about fifteen other pregnant couples in New York Hospital. A cute, energetic, and perky young nurse named Karen Mitchell tells us briefly about the hospital, the check-in procedure, and the labor and delivery process.

We are then given stupid-looking yellow paper surgical gowns, which make us look like big chickens, to put on over our street clothes, and we go off on a tour of the maternity wing. We are shown the labor rooms, the birthing room, the delivery room, the nursery, and the private and semi-private rooms. Both private and semi-private rooms are stark and shabby, with paint peeling off the walls and ceilings.

The birthing room, which looks oddly Southern Californian and out-of-place in the austere old Eastern Establishment hospital, features soft lights, pastel colors, an adjustable birthing bed, a stereo, and a better-looking TV than in the other rooms. If you want to use the birthing room, we are told, it must first, of course, be vacant. You must be dilated at least 4 centimeters and express at least an *intention* to do the delivery without drugs. We fall in love with the birthing room.

We realize we know one of the couples in the tour. Neither they nor we had known the others were expecting. All of the women present are fairly large with child. I note with some satisfaction that there is at least one dad present who looks older than I do.

The more we see, the more frightened both Suzanne and I become, realizing that the next time we come here it will be to go into labor and deliver our own baby.

As we walk through the halls a nurse comes toward us, wheeling a newborn in an enclosed cart. "Baby!" she screams to nobody in particular, "Baby!"

Suzanne shudders.

"It's like a short order cook in a diner," she says.

We are warned repeatedly about bringing valuables into the hospital with us. There has been a lot of theft. Wives are cautioned to leave purses, credit cards, cash, and jewelry at home—even rings. One woman who had had general anesthesia for a Caesarian awoke in the recovery room to find a thief trying to pull her wedding ring off her finger.

Upon leaving the hospital, we stop by the receptionist's desk in the Admissions Office, as we were instructed, to get our pre-registration forms which had never arrived in the mail.

The receptionist, a pudgy woman intent upon watching a

segment of "Dallas," explains with no little irritation that she cannot be expected to provide pre-registration forms to everybody in the hospital who wants them, and gives us a phone number to call tomorrow when another person will be there and when, presumably, "Dallas" will not be on TV.

*

January 11. My friend Joe, a man whom I have known intimately in my therapy group for twelve years, has died of lung cancer. He was, at fifty-three, one of the handsomest, most generous, energetic, and lively men I have ever met.

Joe had two grown children by his first wife, then remarried and decided to have another child with his new young wife. He had brought his baby daughter to group, and I loved seeing them together. Joe's experience with this baby had been a great influence on my decision to become a father myself.

I attend Joe's standing-room-only funeral at Campbell's Funeral Chapel in New York, and I weep for him, his wife, his little daughter, and for myself. I had so much wanted him to meet my son.

*

January 29. To absolutely nobody's surprise, our New York apartment is not ready on this day, when Lamaze classes are due to begin.

Our six Lamaze classes will be held every Tuesday, from 8:00 to 10:00 P.M., on the Upper East Side of Manhattan. They are led by Bertha Webber, an attractive, energetic, and humorous registered nurse and mother of three, who speaks so fast it is almost impossible to take notes.

Our first class is the last group's sixth—our sixth is scheduled so close to our March 17th due date that it is unlikely we'd be able to attend. This class is devoted to baby care and baby products.

Bertha expounds on the relative merits of Snuglis as opposed to cheaper products like the Huggy Bunny; various brands of collapsible "umbrella" strollers like the Aprica and the Maclaren; baby carseats; baby-care books; baby nurses; babysitters; baby bathseats; baby bottles; Nuk nipples and pacifiers; Johnson & Johnson rattles and toys; cloth diapers vs. disposables; playpens with mesh sides; rocking chairs in which to give night feedings; cribs; crib accessories; crib mobiles; supplies to handle the baby's first sickness; discount stores which sell most of the foregoing.

She has specific recommendations about everything. For example, on umbrella strollers: "Don't get one that you can't open and collapse with one hand, since it's an unwritten rule in New York not to help a mother carrying a baby and a load of baby equipment to get on a bus."

On changing tables: "Get some mirrored tiles to put on the wall next to your changing table—your baby will be fascinated by his own image and distracted from playing with his poop and smearing it all over your blouse and your hair."

On crib mobiles: "The only one to buy is the longest-playing windup Fischer-Price Dancing Animals Musical Mobile, because it is the only one that is designed to be looked at from beneath by a baby, and, also, because it will give you seven whole minutes in which to take a shower, wash your hair, blow it dry, and put on some clothes."

On what she calls "the arsenic hour," from 6:00 to 8:00 P.M. when baby is fussy: "Try to change out of your nightgown before your husband comes home so it will look like you've done something during the day."

*

February 4. We are in our eighth month. I have started doing most of our grocery shopping at the East Hampton A&P. It saves Suzanne the trouble, and the market is quite uncrowded at this time of year. It also allows me to check out the cover stories of the tabloids. Here are a sampling of today's tabloid cover stories at the A&P checkout counter, all dated a week ahead, February 12:

"WARNING:
NATURAL CHILDBIRTH CAN BE DANGEROUS,
EVEN FATAL!"

"MOM GIVES SELF A CAESARIAN!"

"SIX WEEK OLD BABY HEALS THOUSANDS!"

"CABBAGE PATCH DOLL STRANGLES MOM!"

The one about natural childbirth is from that bastion of responsible journalism, the *National Enquirer*. The one about the Mom giving herself a cesarian concerned a desperate woman who, for reasons I didn't have time to learn, cut herself open on her kitchen table with a carving knife. I never did get the story about the Cabbage Patch Doll who strangled the Mom, and I'm hoping it wasn't the same Mom who gave herself the cesarian, but if it was, I hope she knew about the six-week-old baby who heals thousands.

I am trying hard not to worry about birth defects and other things that could go wrong with the baby. In the mail today is a letter from the March of Dimes which I did not need to read. It begins:

Dear Friend:
I'll come straight to the point. Each year 250,000 American babies are born with birth defects. And I urgently need your help. That's 1 out of every 12 newborns!
—Some are born with a physical deformity like a missing limb.
—Others are born with metabolic diseases like Tay-Sachs or cystic fibrosis.
—Yet others are born with functional or genetic defects like cerebral palsy or Down's syndrome. . . .

*

February 5, afternoon. The obstetrician's office.

On previous visits here I have been careful to stand in the appropriate place in the examination room—next to Suzanne's head, well above the paper skirt which the nurse drapes around Susanne's naked hips for modesty. Suzanne and I, the visiting team, face Dr. Ryan and his nurse, the home team. Dr. Ryan—a silver-haired gentleman with steel-rimmed spectacles, a dry wit and a soft Irish brogue—sits between Suzanne's thighs, with the nurse behind him and a high intensity lamp beamed over his shoulder while he examines Suzanne's vagina.

This time, because I have decided I want to take a more active role in the pregnancy, I walk around to the other side of the paper skirt to where Ryan is sitting, peering into Suzanne's private parts. Thinking to find out some useful medical information and to sort of be one of the guys, I ask, "What are you looking at?"

Dr. Ryan glances up, startled.

"Who, me?" he replies nervously.

He has obviously heard my words and misunderstood my tone. I look at Suzanne. She is biting down hard on her lip to keep from laughing.

After we leave the office Suzanne says to me:

"That has to be the gynecologist's nightmare-come-true— that someday a husband will actually nail him for looking at and touching his wife's vagina."

I feel incredibly stupid.

*

February 5, evening. Lamaze class #2. A heavy snowstorm has been in progress for two hours. Eight to twelve inches of snow have been predicted before the end of the night. We are not as worried as we might be about returning to East Hampton because our Jeep has four-wheel drive.

This will be our regular Lamaze group, and tonight is its

first meeting. There are thirteen couples, all looking pretty middle class, and most seeming to be in their thirties—one man, as in the hospital tour, is fortunately older-looking than I. The women, of course, all have prominent bellies. Some of the men wear three-piece suits and look like bankers.

Everyone is encouraged to say what he or she is feeling about coming here. One husband says he doesn't know why he's here. Another says he is there under protest. They both get laughs. I think they are assholes.

Bertha says she is self-conscious about calling Lamaze "natural childbirth."

"That conjures up visions of delivering a baby and then going out to work in the rice paddies an hour later." She speaks of natural childbirth among animals. "Cats deliver perfectly—just watch them push out each kitten, give it a bath, and then eat up the afterbirth. We are the only animal that doesn't eat its own afterbirth, and the only animal that doesn't have milk at birth. It is thought that eating the placenta facilitates the immediate production of milk. A group in California has just started experimenting with eating the placenta, so now we'll know. If you don't wish to eat your placentas after your baby's birth, ladies, Lederle Labs will buy it from you for 25 cents.

"Natural childbirth," she says, "is not guaranteed to be painless—it will probably hurt like hell, but the pain is a different kind of pain and it never lasts longer than ninety seconds. Some of you will spend only three hours in labor and the baby will pop right out, and some of you will need C-sections, and you won't know who you are until it happens."

She discusses epidurals—local anesthetics which can be given during delivery:

"Some of you will probably say, 'Listen, just give me my epidural right now and let's forget about the breathing.' " She emphasizes that she doesn't intend to grade everybody in the class on how well they did in labor and how little anesthetic they required.

We discuss breast-feeding, which she recommends, and she announces a two-hour breast-feeding class that we are welcome to attend. She tells us what procedures are followed if the mother does not intend to breast-feed. "They used to give testosterone at birth to non-breast-feeding mothers, but they had to stop that because they found some of them were getting deep voices and facial hair."

Someone asks about episiotomies—the cutting of the skin between the vagina and the rectum during the delivery to prevent tearing the perineum. Bertha says that 96–97 percent of all women delivering first babies have episiotomies.

We are told about the three types of vaginal birth. The easiest delivery is called Vertex, which is head first—96 percent are vertex births. More difficult is Breech birth, which is feet first. There is also Transverse birth, which means that the baby is coming down laterally and must be turned around or else delivered by C-section.

Before the fetus settles to the bottom of the womb it is said to be "floating." As it settles, but before it is lodged firmly in place, it is "dipping." When the fetus lodges at the bottom of the womb, it is "engaged." First babies generally engage two to six weeks before delivery.

"When the baby engages," says Bertha, "your bladder capacity is reduced to half a cup. A kick in the bladder from baby on the bus will make you pee in your pants. If you haven't had that happen yet, ladies, it's coming."

The contractions of labor serve to "efface," or flatten, the mouth of the womb, and to dilate it. Five fingerbreadths, or 10 centimeters (pronounced SAHN-timeters), is fully dilated—when this happens, a nurse will say, "She's *fully*, doctor."

Next we discuss the rupturing of the membranes, or the breaking of the amniotic sac of waters. We learn that 25 percent of women rupture their membranes just before labor begins, 50 percent rupture them during labor, and 25 percent have to have them ruptured by the obstetrician.

"When your water breaks," says Bertha, "it can be only a trickle, or you can lose a quart—nature likes to keep you guessing. But when it happens, a chemical is released which makes you euphoric, so as you're gushing out a quart of water on the carpet in Bloomingdale's Cosmetics Department, you'll have a big smile on your face."

I recall Joan Rivers's routine in which she says that when her water broke it drowned her dog.

Bertha explains bodily changes during pregnancy, using several large charts of the female anatomy in profile. She demonstrates the action of the womb in delivery, utilizing a fuzzy pink woolen bag with a drawstring and a ball—"My mother made this," she says parenthetically.

She simulates the actual delivery, thrusting a baby doll through a pelvic bone. She shows us how the baby's head has to rotate to get through the narrow pelvic opening: the baby looks toward the mother's right hip at the start, then turns face down as its head starts coming out, then looks up as it emerges completely. "Sunnyside up" babies are born upside down—that is, looking up.

We learn about the fontanelle, a soft spot in the top of the baby's skull. During delivery, the bones in the skull contract and can even overlap the fontanelle to enable the head to compress and elongate and pass through the narrow birth canal. This pressure causes some babies to be born with extremely elongated heads—"real cucumber-heads," says Bertha—but it is, happily, only a temporary condition.

At the end of class Suzanne and I tell Bertha we are nervous about being so far out on Long Island as the March 17 delivery date approaches. She recommends that we make contact with an excellent obstetrician at Southampton Hospital. His name is Dr. Fear.

Dr. Fear. A perfect name for somebody for me to consult

about this pregnancy. He sounds like the villain in a James Bond movie.

*

The blizzard is so severe on our drive back to East Hampton after Lamaze class that we can barely see. Cars ahead of us on the unplowed Long Island Expressway frequently skid and slowly spin out—360 degrees in one direction, then 360 in the other. It's all so white and pretty and slow, it looks utterly harmless, but I give them a wide berth, and am confident that our Jeep's four-wheel drive will keep us from skidding.

By the time we reached the unplowed Sunrise Highway two hours later there are no other cars in sight and no markers visible at either side of the road to show where the shoulders are. It seems as though we are just driving across a peaceful white glacier. It is probably dangerous as hell, but I love the sensation and I am almost sad when we finally reach our own snowy driveway two hours later.

The following morning we awake to well over a foot of snow covering everything in sight. It looks so dazzling I step outside and wade through the drifts, snapping pictures of the house that I have for seventeen years known only in the summer and never seen in snow.

There is absolutely no sound as I walk through our muffled woods but the snow crunching—no, creaking—under my boots. In the later afternoon the shadows in the snow are light blue in color. At night the air is so clear and the full moon so bright that when we go to bed I have to get up three times to make sure I haven't left on the outdoor floodlights. I have never seen it this bright at night. It looks just like those day-for-night scenes in movies where they underexpose sunlight to try and make it pass for midnight.

*

February 11, morning. I am at the A&P again, and as I am

unloading onto the checkout counter my four 25-pound bags of Kleen Kitty litter, my three bags of Meow Mix, my six boxes of Tender Vittles, and my forty cans of Friskies Buffet Mixed Grill, another tabloid headline—this on the February 19 edition of the *Sun*—catches my eye:

"PREGNANT MAN GIVES BIRTH!"

Concerned about the sympathetic pregnancy symptoms I have thus far experienced, and unwilling to let another story like the mom who gave herself a Caesarian or the Cabbage Patch strangler go by uninvestigated, I plunk down my fifty cents and get to read the following:

An astonished 27-year-old man recently "gave birth" to what doctors believe should have been his twin brother. Mario Grasso never knew he had the bizarre "infant" growing inside him until just before it was delivered via Caesarian section.

The man grew up in a rural area of Northern Italy and has always been very active in sports. He worked as a carpenter and was in the best of physical condition. Then in March of 1984, he began to feel weak and dizzy a lot of the time. He became moody and irritable over little things that never bothered him before, and he was gaining weight.

"My wife was pregnant, and she kept telling me I was having sympathy symptoms. That sounded reasonable at first," says Mario with a shrug. "But by July, I looked like I was carrying a watermelon around inside me, and I knew all those extra inches were not from over-eating!"

I will not quote you the whole story, but it goes on to tell how Mario went to a doctor and was diagnosed as having a teratoma tumor, which had "all the characteristics of a real baby: teeth, hair, brain cells, arms and legs." Mario's doctor observed reasonably: "It is certainly one of the most unusual cases I have ever seen."

The tumor was removed and, according to the *Sun*, Mario's wife gave birth to a healthy baby girl just three weeks after Mario's surgery. "If nothing else," said Mario, "this problem has made me much more sensitive to the mood changes and

other problems my wife suffers from during pregnancy . . .
I even went through postpartum blues after my tumor was
removed."

I am able to forget about Mario Grasso until my next trip to
the A&P on February 19. As I am lifting more 25 pound sacks
of Kleen Kitty out of my shopping cart, I notice the February
26 edition of the *Sun*, whose lead story is:

"Nurses faint, Doctors Reel in Horror As . . .
DEVIL BABY BORN WITH HORNS!"

Relatively unthreatened by babies born with horns, I am
just about to take out my checkbook and pay for the groceries,
when I spot the February 26 edition of the *National Examiner*:

"Doctor's Astonishing Revelation:
YOUR HUBBY COULD BECOME PREGNANT!"

Anxieties about Mario Grasso successfully repressed for
a week erupt afresh. I nervously scoop up the *Examiner*.
On page 19 is the same headline again, accompanied by a
big black-and-white photo of a smiling woman with her
arm around a man with a passing resemblance to Jim Nabors,
who is wearing a three-piece suit, a pair of wire-rimmed
glasses, a big smile, and an even bigger belly. The story begins
as follows:

It's just as easy for a man to get pregnant as his mate, say two top
gynecological researchers.

Drs. Richard Harding and Geoffry Thorburn say that it is biologically
possible for a man to carry a fetus, fertilized in a laboratory dish, in his
abdomen for nine months and give birth to a healthy baby. . . .

I think I'm safe.

*

February 11, afternoon. Our eighth month of pregnancy.

Suzanne tacks a roll of white seamless paper to the bedroom wall, sets up her Nikon on a tripod, takes off all her clothes, and begins photographing herself. It is something she has been planning to do for months.

I had been planning to go off on another dozen urgent errands in East Hampton, but, looking at her like this, I am suddenly struck by her beauty. I offer to take the photos instead of having her use the automatic timer.

The more I look at her through the lens the more I am moved. Until that moment I had not really understood what people meant when they said that pregnant women were beautiful or that they seemed to glow. Now I understand.

It has to do with the exaggeration of such female shapes as breasts. It also has to do with the sensual and narcissistic feeling that pregnant women seem to have about their bodies—or, anyway, that *this* pregnant woman has. It is a self-satisfaction that does not depend upon verification by an outside source, and so the outside source is more inclined to verify it.

"My God, but you are an astonishingly beautiful woman," I say.

We have been told it is possible to make love to a pregnant woman until her cervix begins to dilate. Suzanne's cervix has not begun to dilate. We complete the photos and tumble into bed to make love, being careful not to crush the baby.

*

February 12. Terrible Tuesday. Torrential rains and gale force winds. Just before we leave East Hampton for our day in New York, our contractor telephones us in a panic—the plumbers have accidentally cut through a pipe. As a result, water is gushing out, flooding our apartment and that of our downstairs neighbor, Larry Albert. The shutoff valve is in Larry's apartment, but they can't find Larry's key where I left it in our hall closet.

I telephone Larry at work in Connecticut and give him the cheery news. His only hope of preventing his apartment from being turned into a swimming pool is to reach his sister in Manhattan and have her let the plumbers in with her key.

By the time Suzanne and I arrive in New York, the water has been shut off. Our apartment, already in a sorry state, looks not much worse for the flood, but Larry's carpets are drenched and billowing upward, and his ceilings have huge blisters in the plaster billowing downward.

Later in the day, Suzanne phones me in tears at my therapist's office—her wallet, with all her credit cards and I.D and $200 in cash, has been stolen.

As she was entering Bloomingdale's, at 59th and Third Avenue, two men were blocking the revolving door. One, a well-dressed black man, was pretending to have extreme difficulty closing his umbrella. A second, an equally well-dressed white man, apparently unzipped her purse in the confusion and withdrew her wallet and the vinyl banana she used as a coin purse. She has had to borrow a quarter to telephone me.

I leave my therapist's office and rush home to help Suzanne cancel as many credit cards on the phone as we can before the stores close.

Later we tell our friend Leslie Newman about the wallet. She says she's had three of hers stolen at Bloomingdale's. We tell her about the flood. "Well," she says, "now that your water's broken, the baby could come at any time."

*

February 12, evening. Tonight in Lamaze class we will begin to learn the techniques of Lamaze relaxation and breathing.

The principle sounds valid—that concentration upon exaggerated breathing rhythms block the pathway to the brain normally taken by pain, and consequently few pain messages can get through the traffic jam. I am not convinced it will work, but I do not voice my reservations, not wanting to appear negative. At best Lamaze instruction will be helpful, at worst amusing.

Bertha asks for a volunteer for a demonstration. Suzanne raises her hand. Bertha has Suzanne lie down on the floor and relax completely. Then Bertha raises each of Suzanne's limbs, instructing her to let them go limp. Utterly drained from stolen wallets and flooded apartments, Suzanne is quite limp indeed.

"*Very* good," says Bertha.

Next Bertha has all the women lie down on the carpet, their heads on pillows. The men are to instruct their wives to contract various limbs and test the others for relaxation, as Bertha has done with Suzanne.

We are taught to tell our wives to take a deep cleansing breath and then breathe deeply from the chest for a period of 60 seconds. We time the minute on our watches, calling out: "Contraction begins . . . 15 seconds . . . 30 seconds . . . 45 seconds . . . 60 seconds, contraction ends—take a deep cleansing breath." During the breathing our wives are taught to practice "effleurage"—light fingertip massage of their bellies—to remove the temptation to clench their fists during the actual contractions.

Bertha discusses the length of labor: "Some women try to scare you. They'll say, 'Oh, I was in labor eight days and nights.' That's nonsense—if they were in labor that long, it would have killed the mother, the father, the doctor, and everybody else."

We discuss anesthetics and analgesics. We learn that a "caudal" is an injection in the buttock that lasts one hour. An "epidural" is an injection at the base of the spine which also lasts one hour, but when it is given a tiny plastic tube is inserted into the skin. Through this tube more painkiller can be injected every hour.

The danger of epidurals is that they take away the desire to push. Although she teaches Lamaze childbirth, Bertha had to have some form of anesthetic in all three deliveries of her own children.

We learn about the various stages of labor. Stage I she calls Entertainment, because the best way to get through it, she says, is for the husband to entertain his wife. This stage lasts about six to eight hours and features irregular contractions. Dilation in Stage I is 0 to 3 centimeters.

Stage II of labor is called Active, lasts three to four hours, and features regular contractions about three minutes apart. Dilation during Active labor is from 3 to 8 centimeters.

Stage III of labor is called Transition, and lasts about an hour. Dilation during transition is from 8 to 10 centimeters. The contractions last 60 to 90 seconds and are 60 to 90 seconds apart. It is the most painful stage:

"This is the stage, ladies, where you will say, "Look, I changed my mind, forget it, I'll come back next year, I'm not going through with this—cut my head off, I don't care." Stage IV of labor is called Pushing, and lasts 10 to 30 minutes. First the baby is pushed out, and then the placenta.

Bertha tries to impress upon us the need for relaxation during labor, explaining that when you are tense you dump adrenalin into your bloodstream, and adrenalin is a cervical constrictor. If you believe you have started labor, Bertha instructs us, have a glass of wine. If the contractions go away, the labor was false.

*

It had seemed to us that having a baby would be a lot more fun and permit us time to pursue our careers if we had a live-in person to assist with the baby. Live-in American nannies get upwards of $250 a week, but foreigners charge considerably less. A friend named Susan Calhoun Moss, who has an Australian nanny for her baby, recommends our registering with a personnel agency in Vancouver. She thinks we can get a qualified young person with some training for as little as $100 a week.

We fill out the agency's forms and write up a five-page letter describing ourselves, our life, and what we require in a nanny. The agency in Vancouver specializes in Australians, New Zealanders, and British, but they also, for some reason, place Americans with Americans.

The agency sends us material—resumes, letters of recommendation, and photos—on three American girls from the Northwest section of the country, and two Canadian girls from British Columbia. They are all about 20 years old, and untrained.

One of them, Janet, is currently working as a video jockey in Spokane, Washington. From her photo she looks absurdly pretty, but her bio says she smokes, and so we scratch her off the list.

Another, Alison, lives in Idaho, has little experience with small children, but has taken care of a quadriplegic, and also worked for a doctor . . . as a sheepherder.

A third, Donna, has had a few years of working with children, especially newborns, and sounds more promising. We speak to her in British Columbia by phone—she's trained, self-possessed, much more expensive than we'd planned on ($250 a week), and, besides, she has already accepted another position.

I telephone two nanny agencies in New York which have come fairly well recommended. One agency brags that they've placed a nanny with Arthur Schlesinger, another with Jane Pauley. They are appalled at how little we want to pay. Their nannies *start* at $250 a week, and that's the *in*experienced ones. The experienced ones, they say, get $400. They promise to start sending us applicants, but that is the last we hear from either of them.

We learn from Vancouver about an Australian nanny in Manhattan whose British friend is, unbeknownst to her current employers, thinking of leaving her job. Her employers have had a second baby, and, if that weren't bad enough, they are also thinking of moving to the suburbs, which is a bit too far away from the hot pink center for the British nanny's taste.

The British nanny, although only twenty-two, has had several years of experience with newborns, which makes her sound appealing. We also like the fact that she is already working in the city, presumably knows her way around town, and—unlike all the other women we're considering—could be interviewed in person before she's hired.

The Australian friend of the British nanny balks at giving us her friend's phone number, since her friend's employers aren't aware she's considering leaving. She also refuses to give us her friend's name. She even declines to give us *her* name. All she will do is take messages for her friend and have her friend call us.

After numerous missed connections, the British nanny reaches us by phone and we have a longish chat. She is willing to reveal that her name is Cathy. She has a cockney accent, is extremely energetic and animated, and sounds rather more independent than we'd hoped. She makes it plain that she is not happy we spend so much time in East Hampton, that she gets weekends off and spends them at a friend's house, that she doesn't like to be cooped up in the house, that she is not happy to hear that we work at home and would be there when she is working, that she is taking off the month of August to drive with her Australian friend to California.

Despite all of the above, she *is* the only real lead we've got who has experience with small children, and she *is* the only person so far whom we'd actually be able to meet before hiring. We arrange to meet her on February 16, right after the baby shower that some of Suzanne's friends are throwing for her.

The Vancouver agency puts us in touch with an American

girl named Colleen who lives just outside Seattle. Colleen is only twenty, but she sounds very nice and very flexible, and she charges only $75 to $100 a week. She appears to be a better bet than Cathy.

Then the Vancouver agency tells us about Karen, a nurse from New Zealand who has had nanny training and who is currently finishing up a job in Toronto. Karen is the only nanny the agency currently handles who has been specifically trained to work with very small children.

We telephone Karen in Toronto and chat for about an hour. She sounds exactly what we are looking for—she is experienced with newborns, loves animals, has no reservations about babysitting, and sounds quite flexible. She has a lovely accent. There is just one small problem: She is just about to accept a position with two families in Canada.

We are appalled to discover somebody who sounds so perfect and to find her already taken.

Suzanne and I put on a full-court press. We point out how much less work it would be for her to take care of just one baby than to take care of the children of two families in Canada.

We seduce her with descriptions of our apartment in midtown Manhattan, which is four blocks from St. Patrick's Cathedral and Saks Fifth Avenue and the United Nations and I don't know what else, with descriptions of our East Hampton house and its swimming pool and how we are only a five-minute drive from the beach, with the knowledge that we would take her and the baby with us to Los Angeles anytime we went to shoot a movie, as we did two years ago for *Private School*, or to ski in Colorado, as we've been doing for the past couple of winters.

She seems impressed, but expresses reservations about New York.

We proceed to sell her New York in a way that makes the "I Love New York" commercials look understated by comparison. We make it sound like we spend every available moment atop the Empire State Building or the World Trade Center, or attending exhibits at the Metropolitan or the Museum of Modern Art, or taking horse-drawn cabs to plays on Broadway and concerts at Carnegie Hall.

She says it all sounds very exciting, but she is a naive New Zealander who was raised on a ranch and she isn't used to such a fast pace.

We switch tactics immediately and point out how, although we are so *close* to all of these exciting things in New York, we are such homebodies we seldom even go out of the apartment, which just happens to be *extremely* well-insulated for sound and *very* quiet, and on one of the quietest blocks in Manhattan, and that our house in East Hampton, where we spend *so* much time, is in the woods and so still and peaceful that we sometimes get really annoyed at the birds for making such a racket.

Nothing of what we've told her is untrue. However, it occurs to me that what we are doing is seductive, faintly sexual, and utterly shameless. But it seems to work. She seems dizzied by our onslaught. She says she will think over all we have told her and will call us back the following evening.

We spend an exceedingly anxious twenty-four hours, agonizing over what we will do if Karen turns us down, and then Karen calls back. She says she has really thought about it, and although she has not definitely made up her mind, she was very impressed by what we told her and is anxious to come to work for us.

We are very glad and extremely relieved, but now a very peculiar and embarrassing reaction sets in for both us—even though Suzanne and I are on extensions of the phone several rooms apart, I know her well enough to read her feelings. We have invested so much energy in trying to win her away from the other couples that the victory is somewhat anticlimactic. It is a reaction I sometimes experienced in my dating days, when hotly pursuing a particularly attractive and elusive woman, and then suddenly winning her.

I sense both of us pulling back from Karen and examining our reservations. For example: Can we really hire Karen to come and live with us for at least a year and take care of our baby and become part of our family, based on just two telephone conversations? It is like sending away for a mail-order bride. Can we really take on Karen without at least interviewing Cathy, the one person we are able to meet?

We tell Karen that we are inclined to hire her—all we want to do is have her send us her references, and interview the British nanny on Saturday in New York, and then we'll let her know our decision. She says fine, but I hang up the phone feeling like a cad. Here we have seduced this poor girl away from a rather prosaic job with honest people of Canada, and now we don't even know if we want her.

✳

February 16. After the baby shower at the home of our friends Bob Berkowitz and Merrilee Cox, we interview Cathy the British nanny.

Cathy is a young British Bette Midler. She has bright red hair in a short semi-punk hairdo, tight black jeans, a pink jacket, lots of energy, and an accent vaguely reminiscent of Mick Jagger. She seems more like a rock singer than a nanny. When we ask how she would feel about regularly taking over one of the nighttime feedings for the first few months, she is appalled.

"It would just make me cranky the following day," she says.

We ask how she'd feel about babysitting a few nights a week. She seems similarly disquieted by this notion, but appears to be making a conscious decision not to seem too negative on a job interview.

"Well, I mean, what time would you be getting home?" she says. "Do you think it would be by 1:30?"

Realizing she is legitimately concerned about staying up that late when she has to get up early the following morning to help with the baby, we reassure her that we would never be getting home later than 1:30 A.M.

"Well," she says, "I wouldn't mind that so much, then. As long as you were back by 1:30, I could still go dancing at a disco."

Cathy reveals that she dropped out of school at the age of sixteen, has been a nanny in England, Canada, and New York, and that she has never remained anywhere longer than a year.

"Why did you become a nanny?" asks Suzanne, hoping for some uplifting answer like, "Because I love children so much."

"Why did I become a nanny?" Cathy repeats, and thinks about this for a moment. "I guess for the travel."

There are many good answers to Suzanne's question. This has not been one of them.

Karen's references arrive in the mail and look superb. No American agency has sent us a single applicant to consider. We phone Cathy and Colleen and express our regrets, then we call Karen and tell her she has the job.

*

February 17. When we first learned we were pregnant in late June, numerous friends with small children offered us their outgrown baby beds and carseats and playpens and Snuglis and baby clothes. When we called back a few months later, we were told that these friends had just given away all their things or else changed their minds and decided to keep them. "Don't you want to buy your own things?" said many of them in a rather patronizing manner.

We felt like beggars and we were embarrassed. Only Jill Krementz and Kurt Vonnegut, who are more acquaintances than friends, actually came up with a baby carseat, a playpen, and a bassinet.

And so it is that, on Sunday, February 17, a day after the baby shower, we go down to the Lower East Side, to the three discount stores that were recommended to us in Lamaze class, to buy baby furniture.

Our first stop is at Ben's Babyland, at 87 Avenue A. A sign on the wall at Ben's Babyland reads: "We deliver everything . . . but the baby."

Ben himself is short, stocky, handsome, and roughly sixty years of age. He has gray hair and wears a sportcoat, an open-necked shirt, gold chains, and gold Porsche glasses. He maintains a bemused and amusing air—a Borscht Belt comedian more than a businessman. He tells me he's been in this business forever. He started working in his father's store when he was still a kid. I ask him about the Maclaren stroller.

"The Maclaren is a good fifty dollar stroller," he says. "Unfortunately, it costs a hundred and twenty dollars."

He goes on to say that the Maclaren is "tippy"—lightweight and unsteady—and that you couldn't give 'em away in the suburbs, where they don't care about lightness of weight or ease of folding like they do in the city.

We ask Ben's opinion on baby car seats. He gives us a spiel on the brand he recommends, the Strolee.

We ask Ben's opinion on mattresses. He says there are three kinds: foam, hair, and inner-spring.

"Is the hair horse hair?" I ask.

"It's not horse hair, it's *hog's* hair," says Ben. "Lots of stores will tell you it's horse hair. What's *horse* hair? It's soft, just like ours, it's *nothing*. Get the hog's hair or the inner-spring—the foam is junk."

We look at a few baby beds and find it quite difficult to put their sides either up or down. We ask Ben how you put a baby into a crib whose side needs two hands to put it up or down.

"Easy," says Ben. "You just fling the baby up into the air, release the side, then catch him on the way down. Either that or you put the baby on the floor."

We try to work a two-handed crib, and can't, and decide it

must be a three-handed crib. We try to work a one-handed crib—or, actually, a one-hand-and-one-foot crib—and fail at that as well, lifting the rail with one hand and kicking away fruitlessly at the release lever below it. Ben is vastly amused at our ineptness.

Our next stop is Schachter's, 81 Avenue A, at 5th Street. Miraculously, Ben is at Schachter's too, expounding on baby furniture to a customer. Ben turns out to own the more expensively priced Schachter's as well as Ben's Babyland.

Suzanne notices a white French crib she likes, and is surprised to find out it costs $5.00 more here, in a Lower East Side discount store, than the same item at the Au Chat Botte, a very fancy store on Madison Avenue. She asks a tall, heavyset gentleman named John, who appears to manage the store, about this oddity. John gets very upset with her and says he doesn't know or care what *other* stores charge, this is what *Schachter's* charges.

When John has calmed down, we ask if we can buy a crib now and have him hold it in the store till our New York apartment is finished being renovated.

"If you give me a deposit," says John, "I'll hold the crib till the kid is in *college.*"

We are reassured, secretly fearing that the renovation may not be completed until that point in our baby's life.

"One woman gave me a hundred dollar deposit on a crib about a year ago," John continues, warming to his subject, "and I can't even find her to give it to her. I don't know what happened to her—maybe she died—but I'd sure like to get rid of it."

We ask if we can write him a check, and he agrees.

"But when the check bounces," he says, "we come for the baby."

We go next to Schneider's, 20 Avenue A, between East Houston and East 2nd Street. The prices at Schneider's seem to be a trifle lower than Ben's, and the merchandise is more densely packed into the store—rocking chairs stand on top of cribs, and so on.

I ask a Schneider's salesman about the Aprica versus the Maclaren stroller. The salesman snorts, points to the Aprica, and insists I look at a warning label sewn into the back of the stroller.

"Read that last paragraph there," he insists. "It's a joke."

I read the last paragraph. It says: "The stopper is designed to function normally as long as the stroller is empty. Do not place too much confidence in it when the stroller is loaded with baby or luggage."

We approach Schneider himself, an abrasive, angry, but knowledgeable man of about sixty, who sports a day's growth of beard, a fedora, and a down vest. We ask Schneider about mattresses, and he is as vehemently in favor of foam as Ben was against it, swearing that hair mattresses leave indentations when kids jump on them, and that most hair mattresses hardly have any hair in them anyway:

"You got so little hair in a mattress like that," he says, caught up in his own words, "you don't even got enough that I could choke on it. They just fill it with foam and then they throw a little hair on the top."

We ask Schneider about the Strolee baby carseat which Ben had recommended over all others. Schneider tells us he prefers the Safe & Sound II over the Strolee, and demonstrates how much more quickly a baby can be buckled into it:

"You'll start putting your baby into the Strolee," says Schneider, "*I'll* be halfway there with the Safe & Sound before you finish."

We ask Schneider about rockers to sit in while nursing the baby during night feedings.

"You see that rocker over there?" says Schneider. "That's a Canadian rocker. It's the only good thing they make in Canada—the rest is junk. We got a load of stuff in here from Canada the other day, I sent it right back. It was all junk."

Perhaps fearing we do not believe him, he turns suddenly to an elderly salesman at the other end of the store and yells to him: "You remember that shipment we got in from Canada the other day? What did we do with it?"

"Sent it right back," corroborates the obedient salesman. Schneider appears exonerated.

"It was pure junk," he repeats.

We tell Schneider we've heard that the Maclaren stroller is big in Manhattan but doesn't sell in the suburbs because it's tippy. He appears to take this as a personal affront.

"Look," he says.

He sets the brake on a Maclaren stroller and backs it up against the counter. He takes a heavy metal bill-of-sale writing box off the counter and places it on the awning of the stroller.

"Didn't tip over, did it?" he says.

We admit it didn't. He puts another heavy metal bill-of-sale writing box on top of the first.

"Still didn't tip over, did it?" he says.

We concede that it didn't. He spreads his hands, as if he has made his case for all eternity. I am not certain what this demonstration has proven, other than that if you set the brake on a Maclaren stroller and back it up against a counter, you can put two heavy metal bill-of-sale writing boxes on its awning. It is probably not a situation that comes up much in the life of your average mom or pop.

We end up buying the Maclaren stroller, the French crib, the Safe & Sound II car seat, the Fisher-Price Dancing Animals Musical Mobile, and a lot of other stuff. The total is well over $1,000.

*

February 19, afternoon. Since nobody knows which of the four obstetricians in Dr. Ryan's practice will be on duty when Suzanne's labor starts, it is Ryan's custom to have all of his partners examine his patients in their final month of pregnancy.

Today it is Dr. Steadman. Dr. Steadman is a tall, white-haired, friendly, and energetic man. He examines Suzanne and at first fears that the baby is too small. Then he realizes it is positioned farther down than he thought, and it is therefore medium-sized. We are considerably relieved.

Trying out our newly learned jargon, we ask: "Is the fetus dipping or engaged?"

"Dipping," replies Dr. Steadman, obviously impressed with our medical vocabulary, "and practically engaged."

We tell him our New York apartment is being renovated and will not be ready for the baby's due date, but that we are going to reserve a room in a nearby hotel. We ask how much before due date we need to move into the hotel.

"Well, normally we like to have you no more than twenty-five miles away in the last six weeks of pregnancy," he says, "but if the pregnancy proceeds as well as it seems to be going, you can wait till a week before. And in an emergency you can always go to Southampton. Southampton Hospital is a very good place—it's staffed by a lot of doctors who interned at New York Hospital. If you were in the middle of the island, I would tell you to move back to the city right now."

*

February 19, evening. We begin tonight's Lamaze class by viewing a film on cesarian sections. In it various moms of all ages, body types, and ethnic affiliations tell about their C-sections in a rap group. Obstetrical surgeons describe the operation, including various ways to make the incision (the old-fashioned vertical Mid-line incision or the newfangled horizontal Bikini incision). There is actual footage of women going into the O.R., having their bellies sliced open and surgeons plucking tiny red scowling babies out of them. I am a person who has great difficulty in crying—the most I can get is one tiny tear in each eye—but every time a baby is born in the film, my eyes fill with water.

The newborns seem not to be handled with great tenderness in the delivery room, and when the film is over Suzanne tells Bertha she finds this upsetting. Bertha is a bit defensive about how newborns have to be bathed, weighed, measured, footprinted, and so on, but Suzanne is not reassured.

Bertha says that the staff at New York Hospital is willing to do anything within reason to accommodate parents' wishes when the baby is born, and tells of a young father who insisted upon playing a flute when his son was delivered because he wanted that to be the first sound the baby heard.

Bertha describes how the baby is given to the father to hold while the mother is being sewn up, then put on the mother's belly for bonding. She admits that the length of time the baby is permitted to remain on the mother's belly has to do with how busy they are: "Bond quickly," she parodies them, "we need this room in twenty minutes."

She tells why dads aren't allowed to stay during C-sections if the mom is put under general anesthesia: "We put a tube down your throat, we put tape over your eyes, we do some very unattractive things to you during general anesthesia, and that is why we don't let husbands into the room when we're doing a cesarian."

We practice our deep chest breathing. "Remember," says Bertha, "you don't start your breathing until you can't walk, talk, or joke."

We learn Phase II breathing: a series of short, shallow pants, accented 1-2-3-4, 1-2-3-4. While our wives do the breathing, we are to pant along with them in order to set the rhythm, calling out the time every fifteen seconds, and squeezing their closest knee for the middle part of the timed minute to simulate the pain of the contraction.

The panting is supposed to produce a sound like "HEE-hee-hee-hee, HEE-hee-hee-hee . . ." Bertha instructs the class to pant this way in unison, the men as well as the women. We sound like a pack of whispering hyenas.

Next Bertha gives us some information to prevent our having anxiety attacks upon seeing our newborns: Babies are born with elongated heads, from being compressed in the birth canal. Babies are born, "not with the familiar Gerber baby pink complexion, but with a nice oxfordcloth blue skin tone." Baby boys are born with enlarged, puffy scrotums. Girl babies are sometimes born with puffy breasts, which contain what old wives call "witch's milk." Girl babies often have what is called pseudo-menstruation—bloodspots on their diapers. On the third day, most babies get jaundice. All of these things are normal, and nothing to worry about.

Bertha once more recommends that we at least try breast-feeding, citing one particularly interesting fact: Breast-fed babies' poop looks like French's mustard, and doesn't smell at all. Bottle-fed babies' poop looks like Gulden's and smells in the normal manner.

Newborn babies like to focus on things which are twelve inches away, and they prefer images of faces to anything else. Squeezing a newborn will make him feel like he's back in the womb and will reassure him.

Bertha recommends staying in the hospital for four days: "On the fourth day your milk starts, your breasts look like Dolly Parton, and you will have your first bowel movement."

*

February 21, morning. I realize my fears have returned. The baby is due in less than four weeks, and the fears I have had—about birth defects, about the ways in which the baby will change our lives—did not go away, I had merely repressed them, pushed them down in some place that I couldn't look at them, for fear of being inappropriate, for fear that they would open up and swallow me whole.

The pregnancy, which had seemed so unreal and which had been going along slowly, has started speeding up and up, and now it is like the runaway train in the movie *Silver Streak*—brakes gone, hurtling out of control, soon to reach the end of the track and smash through the wall of the station. Suzanne told me last night she was afraid.

"Of what?" I said, but I knew.

On previous occasions we had been quick to discuss and analyze our fears about the birth and the health of the baby in good therapeutic tradition. This time we were so close to the moment of truth that neither of us was particularly anxious to discuss the matter further. Instead we practiced our Stage I and II breathing, and I tried to simulate the pains of contractions by squeezing her knee as we had been taught, aware that the pain of squeezed knees had about as much relation to the pain of childbirth as the sting of a horsefly had to the impact of a .44 magnum bullet.

As always when we are both afraid of something, I pretend that I am not worried and that things will be OK. I feel it is my duty as the man of the family. I do not think it fools her, but she generally chooses to behave as though she finds it comforting.

*

February 21, afternoon. I go to Saks to buy a refill of the Clarins oil we bought in Paris for Suzanne to rub on her belly to prevent stretchmarks.

Not surprisingly, what cost $8 in Paris costs $22 at Saks. A Hispanic saleswoman with a wispy moustache waits on me.

"Is your wife pregnant?" she asks.

I say yes, she's due in March.

I'm due in May," says the saleswoman, and I feel a sudden strong kinship with her.

"Is it your first?" she asks.

I say it is.

"Me too," she says.

"It's exciting, isn't it?" I say.

She smiles and says it is.

"It's also scary," I add, thinking of all the terrible things that can go wrong with pregnancies.

Her smile flickers.

"You can't think about that," she replies.

I pay for the Clarins oil and we wish each other good luck. There are tears in my eyes, and I have a curious urge to hug her, but I don't, and instead merely wave and leave the store.

*

February 25. In my sleep I am aware of Suzanne stirring beside me in bed, and then I hear her voice:

"Uh-oh," she says.

I am instantly awake.

"What is it?" I say, knowing what the answer will be.

"I think I'm having contractions," she says.

I reach for my watch. It is 4:54 A.M.

"Let's start timing them," I say, the calmness of my voice belying the terror that has dumped a quart of adrenalin into my veins and started my heart hammering in my chest. This is only our eighth month of pregnancy. The baby isn't due till March 17. If it comes now it will be premature.

Suzanne calls out the beginning and end of each contraction and I note the times on a little pad. The contractions are at first fairly irregular, three to seven minutes apart, and Suzanne is faintly apologetic.

"I hope we're not timing gas pains," she says.

Bertha, our Lamaze teacher, advises anybody who thinks she's in labor to have a glass of wine—if the wine stops the contractions, it's false labor. Suzanne has a glass of wine. The contractions don't stop, they begin to get regular, six minutes apart, forty-five seconds in duration. This is it. Here comes baby, ready or not.

Well, I think to myself, trying to look on the bright side, at least there won't be much traffic on the Long Island Expressway at 5:00 A.M. With luck, we could be at New York Hospital in two hours.

Continuing to time her contractions, I take out a suitcase and begin feverishly packing. Suzanne reminds me that we have not yet learned Pushing or Phase III breathing in Lamaze, but she thinks the Jane Fonda cassette covers this somewhere toward the end of the tape. She turns on the video recorder and tries to find the right section.

Dr. Ryan had said that, were we in New York, we needn't call him till the contractions are regular every five minutes, but since we are in East Hampton to call him whatever their frequency. It has been an hour since the contractions began. I telephone Ryan's office, and a tired, female Brooklyn voice answers.

"This is Suzanne O'Malley's husband—she's an OB patient of Dr. Ryan's and she's just gone into labor," I say.

"How far apart are her contractions?" says the voice.

"Is this the office or the answering service?" I say.

"The office doesn't open till 9:00," says the voice. "This is the service. How far apart are her contractions?"

"Uh, well, they're about six minutes apart," I say self-consciously, "but we're a two- or three-hour drive from the city and the doctor said to call him no matter what their frequency."

"How long ago did the contractions start?" says the voice.

"Uh, about an hour," I say.

"Has her water broken yet?"

"Not yet," I say, aware of the lunacy of having such a discussion with an answering service operator, "but I would like to speak to one of the doctors."

"Has there been a bloody show?" asks the answering service. Although it sounds like British slang, "bloody show" is an obstetrical term which refers to the discharge of the mucus plug from the cervix.

"There hasn't been a bloody show, but I really would like to speak to one of the doctors," I say, having a fantasy that we will arrive at the hospital to find the lady from the answering service scrubbed and waiting to deliver the baby. I am put on hold for a couple of minutes, and then the voice returns.

"I have reached Dr. Martens," she says. "He wants your wife to go to Southampton Hospital to be evaluated by Dr. Fear."

I thank her and hang up without bothering to inform her that we were in contact with Dr. Fear's office a week ago and were told that this week he would be on vacation.

I continue packing, as Suzanne calls out the beginning and end of each contraction so I can make notes on a little pad. When I have thrown enough clothes and washing utensils for a week into my suitcase, it strikes me that Suzanne is being strangely silent in the bathroom. I go into the bathroom to find her sitting on the floor. What she is doing is waxing her legs and underarms.

By the time Suzanne is showered, waxed, and packed, two-and-a-half hours have elapsed, and the contractions have stopped. The excitement of an imminent delivery has given way to extreme fatigue. I am so grouchy I do not trust myself to speak. We agree that we should still go to Southampton to be evaluated, but that there is no longer much urgency.

We sit on the bed, pondering our next move, and soon we have both fallen asleep in our clothes.

We awake in mid-afternoon and go to Southampton. A kindly elderly obstetrician named Dr. Halsey examines Suzanne and says that her cervix is slightly effaced from the contractions, but tight as a drum. There is no need to do anything but go home.

We are fatigued and depressed by a tremendous sense of anticlimax. There is nothing to do now but wait. Contractions could start again tonight, tomorrow, or in three weeks. Until they start again we will be living out of suitcases.

On the way back from Southampton we stop off at the discount drugstore to buy supplies which have been recommended to us in Lamaze class, like a hot water bottle to ease back labor, a spray atomizer to keep Suzanne's mouth moist during the exaggerated breathing, and so on. I muse silently about how long this pregnancy could go on, then notice the lead story in the March 12 edition of the *Weekly World News*:

"MOM PREGNANT FOR 61 YEARS—Child was Conceived in 1924—Mummified Fetus Found in 85-year-old! Exclusive Interview with Doctor!"

*

February 26. In our Lamaze class tonight Bertha informs us in greater detail about Phase III of labor, Transition:

"Up until now, gentlemen, the labor has been going well, and your wife has been delightful. You mop her brow, and she says 'Thank you, darling.' During transition her behavior will change markedly. You will go to mop her brow and she will say, 'Don't touch me! Keep away from me!'

"At this point, ladies," Bertha continues, "the pressure of the baby's head on your rectum will make you feel like you need to move your bowels. You will say to the nurse 'Where-is-the-bathroom-could-you-please-tell-me-where-the-bathroom-is-immediately!' This is why I recommended saying yes when the nurse asked you if you wanted an enema—so you will know what you're pushing out is a baby and not a bowel movement.

"It is at this point, ladies, that you may also feel like you need to vomit. If you had the Mamma Leone dinner before coming to the hospital, this is when it will reappear."

Transition usually takes about an hour, pushing the baby out about half an hour. "Two-thirds of the women in this world squat to deliver their babies," says Bertha. "Unfortunately, we have no obstetricians at New York Hospital who are willing to lie down on the floor to deliver you. The delivery process, unfortunately, is very poorly planned. At the *beginning* of labor is when you have the energy to push, not at the end."

We learn how to do Stage III breathing: panting, as in Stage II, but interspersed with a whistle or a blow.

We learn the technique of Pushing: All the women get

down on the floor and lean against their partners' knees. The woman then grabs her ankles, leans forward, and takes three deep breaths at her partner's direction. She holds the third breath and pushes down three times, then she takes a fast "exchange breath," and pushes again.

"You should feel flushed in the face and like you're going to urinate on the rug—those are the two sensations you want," says Bertha.

"During the actual delivery, gentlemen, you stand at her head, you do not saunter down to discuss the instruments with the obstetrician."

I feel this is intended for me personally, that somehow Bertha has been told of my unintentional harassment of Dr. Ryan in the examination room.

Next we have another film, this one on vaginal delivery. Unlike the previous one on cesarians, this one is in black-and-white, was shot with a hand-held camera, and made about twenty years ago.

In the opening sequence of the film, the pregnant mom who is soon to go into labor is standing in a moving subway car.

"This movie is very realistic," whispers Suzanne. "You'll notice nobody is offering her a seat."

The movie, for all its 1960's quaintness, is fairly affecting, and, needless to say, when the woman's baby is born, I once more find myself in tears. Will Suzanne's delivery be as easy as those in the films, where pink rubber dollies are effortlessly plucked from their calm mom's crotches, or will Suzanne be shrieking in agony while I stand helplessly by? We shall know the answers rather soon.

When the movie is over, the subject of false labor comes up. We are told that 20 percent of women experience false labor. Suzanne raises her hand and tells of *her* false labor the day before. The members of the class are fascinated and horrified, and keep asking her questions about it.

As we prepare to leave, Bertha tells the husbands that we must urge our wives onward during the delivery. "If you say 'I'll bet it hurts a lot, dear, let's go home,' then it's not going to work."

*

March 2, evening. During the night I have a nightmare and awaken, screaming.

"What is it?" says Suzanne, alarmed.

"A werewolf," I reply, "a werewolf coming into the room!"

We both go back to sleep and Suzanne dreams that I am out in the yard, shooting the heads off baby chickens and turkeys with a revolver.

I think we are both a little on edge.

*

"What hospital are you going to have the baby in?" a male friend inquires.

I tell him New York Hospital, assuming that we have time to get there.

"Oh, you'll like New York Hospital," he says. "They have a great waiting room for the fathers."

I look at my friend blankly. I had told him on several occasions that Suzanne and I are doing Lamaze and that I will be with her in the labor room and in the delivery room, so when would I be using the waiting room for fathers?

Curiously, this is the third friend who has made the same mistake. I can't think where this confusion would come from. Perhaps the old picture of a maternity waiting room, with expectant fathers in their shirtsleeves pacing nervously about the room and filling the ashtrays with cigarettes till a nurse emerges to say "It's a boy!" is just too strong to die.

*

Another trip to the A&P, another opportunity to scan the tabloids for things to worry about.

From the March 13 issue of the *Sun*, published the previous week:

"Satan Stole My Unborn Child . . . BABY DISAPPEARS FROM MOM'S WOMB!"

From the March 13 issue of the *National Examiner*: "14-POUND BABY BORN PREGNANT!"

*

March 5, evening. Our final Lamaze class.

We review several subjects, including the breaking of the amniotic sac:

"Dr. Ryan recommends that in your last few weeks of pregnancy you carry a jar of pickles with you at all times," says Bertha. "Then when you water breaks and it starts gushing all over the sidewalk and into your shoes, you just drop your jar of pickles and pretend that's where all this liquid is coming from."

We discuss the advisability of an enema before the delivery, which Bertha recommends. We discuss the shaving of the groin before delivery. Bertha says wives need no longer shave their entire pubic area before going to the hospital. New York Hospital only does a mini-prep now, she says, which means they shave you from the vagina to the rectum. Better yet, if you are a patient of Drs. Ryan, Martens, Steadman, and Schrotenboer, which we are, they do not shave you at all.

We are urged to plan ahead on birth announcements:

"At New York Hospital we do not release your baby unless all your birth announcements are addressed and stamped and ready to mail."

We husbands are given some final advice:

"If your wife calls you at the office and tells you she is having contractions, you go right home, gentlemen, no matter how busy you are, is that clear? If you should awake at some point during the night and find your wife sitting on the bathroom floor doing her transition breathing, you have to take her seriously and do something about it."

And when we get to the hospital and enter Stage III of labor:

"In transition, gentlemen, when your wife says 'I can't do this anymore, I can't stand it!', you must be very firm in getting her to continue her breathing. If you simply say 'Now let's switch to the 6-to-1 breathing, dear,' she will leap out of the East River Drive window of her hospital room."

We are shown a final movie about birth. As each baby emerges from the mother, the sound track plays a burst of religious organ music. I cry on cue at each delivery. There is now such a strong link in me between deliveries and tears, I believe I would cry at the receipt of a special delivery letter.

*

From literature handed out in Lamaze class describing a weekend of workshops for expectant parents at Grossinger's in the Catskills:

Never before in the history of reproduction has it been safer to have a baby. So what are expectant mothers (and fathers) so worried about? Plenty—from accidental early exposure to spermicides, alcohol, aspirin and x-rays, to the cumulative effects of breathing and drinking water in the big city and of eating (PCB contaminated fish, EDB laced citrus and grains, additive-laden groceries) in our modern society. . . .

I stop reading. I had not even *thought* about the cumulative effects of breathing and drinking water in the big city and of eating PCB-contaminated fish, EDB-laden citrus and grains or additive-laden groceries, much less worried about accidental early exposure to spermicides, alcohol, aspirin, and x-rays.

Since the pregnancy began Suzanne has been scrupulously careful about her health. She has always exercised fairly regularly, and when the pregnancy began she bought "Jane Fonda's Pregnancy, Birth, and Recovery Workout" videotape and has been following it faithfully. Her obstetrician told her she can continue whatever level of exercise she is used to, no matter how vigorous, but he advises against skiing—in his opinion, the fetus uses up so much calcium that if Suzanne were to break a bone while skiing it might not set properly.

Suzanne has never been a smoker or coffee drinker. Since the pregnancy she has also eliminated prescription medicines, aspirins, and the megavitamins she was taking every day. This means she is far more vulnerable should she contract a cold, flu, or virus during the pregnancy, and we try with almost pathological zeal to avoid coughers, sneezers, and snifflers in public places. But practically every weekend houseguest we have during the entire pregnancy shows up sick and doesn't bother to inform us until well after the obligatory hugs and kisses of greeting have been implanted.

Despite the best efforts of our houseguests, Suzanne manages to remain well during the pregnancy.

✳

March 6, early morning. We are in our ninth month. We are staying with friends Jeff Brown and Elizabeth Tobin in an apartment that just happens to be four blocks from New York Hospital. This will be our last trip to New York before we move into the Beekman Towers Hotel on March 10 to await the final countdown.

Although Jeff and Elizabeth are not apartment renovators like we are, we are awakened at 8:00 A.M. by the all-too-familiar sounds of three workmen hammering loudly in the next room and tearing up the floor of Jeff's study.

"Construction is a virus," says Suzanne sleepily. "I'm afraid they caught it from us."

✳

March 6, late morning. As we wait for our appointment with Dr. Schrotenboer, I see a big, beautiful blonde mother carrying a big beautiful blonde seven-week-old baby sit down beside us in the waiting room.

I ask her what her baby weighed and how her labor went. She says her baby weighed 9 pounds 3 ounces, and the labor was a breeze—three hours and no pain.

"Was this your first?" I ask, delighted at the possibility that Suzanne's delivery will also be a breeze.

"Oh no, my second."

"And how was your labor with the first one?"

Her expression changes.

"Don't even *ask* about the first one," she says.

Dr. Schrotenboer admits us to her office. She is an extremely pretty, petite blonde in her early thirties. From observing her at a distance on a previous visit, we feared she'd be cold and aloof. On the contrary, she could not be warmer.

Dr. Schrotenboer examines Suzanne and tells her she is dilated 2 centimeters, and that the baby is engaged.

"What does being dilated 2 centimeters mean?" asks Suzanne.

"It means no more baths and no more sex," says Dr. Schrotenboer—either one could now contaminate the fetus. "And it means the baby could come at any time."

"We plan to move into a hotel in town on Sunday," I say. "Do you think the baby will come before Sunday?"

"Not really," she says, "although you never know. I'd say there is only a 20 percent chance it will come before Sunday."

*

March 6, afternoon. Breast-feeding class has been scheduled from 4:00 to 6:00 P.M., but Bertha had warned us that husbands were not welcome during the first hour because a nursing mother was going to give a demonstration.

I get to class about 5:00 to find the nursing mother never arrived because she caught her hand in a door and had to go to the hospital.

There are seventeen women in the room, plus one other guy and me.

Bertha advises the seventeen mothers that they ought to try and nurse the baby for at least six weeks, but not to stop, even if they hate it, till they've done it at least three weeks, because that's how long it takes to make it work and to feel comfortable with it.

We learn that when you're nursing you won't menstruate, but you *can* get pregnant. We learn that when you're nursing and you have an orgasm when you make love, your breasts will leak.

Bertha says that breast-fed babies are never colicky, and wryly mimics a pediatrician on the telephone: "We know that breast-fed babies aren't colicky, so just put the baby on the phone and I'll tell that to him."

We are shown a movie on breast-feeding entitled "The Breastfeeding Experience." In this movie half a dozen moms nurse their babies and talk about their breast-feeding experience.

During the film, I hear Suzanne gasp. Alarmed, I ask what's wrong. She informs me she absentmindedly left a shopping bag at the snack bar she visited before class. Among other things, the bag contained her recently reissued Gold Master-Card that we cancelled when her wallet was stolen in Bloomingdale's.

"I read somewhere that pregnant mothers get more absent-minded as they approach delivery," says Suzanne.

Mmmm, yes. And I'm not going to be the one who calls MasterCard to tell them to cancel that second card, either.

As we exit from the class, we see that a dozen couples from a previous Lamaze class have brought their newborns for the traditional class reunion.

There are about a dozen babies in Maclaren and Aprica strollers and prams and Snuglis, and walking through them in the narrow passageway, my eyes fill up as I pass each one. I guess it's not the deliveries but the babies that make me cry. Walking through this group in the hallway is like walking a gauntlet and being attacked with tear gas.

*

March 6, evening. Before retiring, Suzanne and I practice our Lamaze exercises, as we do most every night. Jeff and Elizabeth ask to watch, and are fascinated. We exaggerate everything because it is a performance.

We go to sleep in the guest room. Sometime during the night Suzanne rouses me. She is sitting up in bed with her thighs spread, and she announces that she is about to deliver the baby.

I scarcely have time to react, when she has a huge contraction and, then, before my astonished eyes, the baby's head emerges from between her legs. I am stupefied. Suzanne does not seem to be at all in pain. The baby's shoulders follow his head, and then the rest of his body emerges, and suddenly there he is—our baby—a little bloody, but completely intact and healthy.

It is an instantaneous and painless delivery, and both Suzanne and I are exultant, overjoyed, and enormously relieved. I can't believe how easy it was, and I can't believe that we didn't even have to go to the hospital.

Suzanne picks the baby up and holds him against her breast, and he begins squirming and wriggling and trying to walk up her chest.

Then the baby turns into a full-grown cat. I realize that I am in the midst of a rather silly dream, and I awake.

*

Thursday, March 7. Shortly after breakfast, Suzanne announces that, in her opinion, the baby is going to be early. We don't have all the things with us that we will need before moving into the hotel on Sunday night, since we had intended to return to East Hampton for the weekend to finish packing. Suzanne says we should go back to East Hampton for just tonight, and then move into the hotel on Friday.

We drive back to East Hampton, making nervous jokes about the fact that we are going the wrong way. As soon as we arrive, we throw ourselves into packing, ensuring that we have enough clothes and supplies for at least two months in case the baby is really late.

While we pack, we watch TV. Interestingly, every program on NBC tonight has references to childbirth: On tonight's episode of "Family Ties," for example, there is a reunion of a Lamaze class. On tonight's episode of "Cheers," Carla, the pregnant waitress, makes jokes about Lamaze. On tonight's episode of "Hill Street Blues," Renko's wife gives birth. Is this an omen or what?

*

Friday, March 8. It *was* an omen. At 5:00 A.M. Suzanne goes into labor. She tries the wine test and the contractions don't stop. She has a shower and wakes me at 7:00, and says it is time to go to New York. I look outside. It is raining heavily.

"Is there time for me to take a shower?" I ask.

No, she says.

"Is there time for me to eat breakfast?"

No, she says.

"Is there time for me to take a poop?"

No, she says.

I throw our bags in the car and we take off in a driving rain, in morning rush hour, for New York.

Suzanne is doing her Lamaze breathing in the car, timing her contractions. I am watching the odometer, trying to be optimistic about the 100 miles we have to go, cheerily announcing the mileage aloud every ten or fifteen miles.

Suzanne seems really afraid that we won't make it. I point out that, if worse comes to worst, we can always head back and go to Southampton Hospital.

"I don't *want* to go to Southampton Hospital," she says like a petulant two-year-old, and then, as frightened as she is, she has to laugh at her childish tone.

The first hour of the trip is fairly fast, with little or no traffic. For the first time in my life I am not afraid of getting a speeding ticket—just like in the movies, a patrol car will pull me over, I'll shout that my wife is in labor, and he will give us a police escort with a siren all the way to the hospital.

One hour out we are already at Exit 60 of the Long Island Expressway, which is halfway there. The Point of No Return.

"Last chance to go to Southampton Hospital and be delivered by Dr. Fear," I say.

Suzanne gives me a wan smile.

Then the traffic, which has been almost non-existent till now, thickens and slows, and soon we are bumper-to-bumper and scarcely moving.

Suzanne is now certain she will have the baby in the car. We have not learned in Lamaze class how to deliver babies in the car, and so I am telling her all kinds of encouraging things, like Stage I of labor lasts a minimum of six to eight hours and we will be there in less than three hours and there is not the slightest chance in the world that she could have the baby in the car even if she wanted to. She isn't buying it.

I had noted on one of our more recent jaunts into New York a Deepdale General Hospital at Exit 32 of the Long Island Expressway. Unfortunately, we are not much past Exit 57 by now, so Exit 32 seems about as far away as New York City. I find myself idly wondering whether police officers really do know how to deliver babies, and I continue helping Suzanne with her Lamaze breathing as I look around for patrol cars.

The traffic begins moving again, and by 10:30 A.M. we arrive at Dr. Ryan's office. We are still in Stage I, as I predicted.

"If Dr. Ryan says this is false labor again," Suzanne confides as we walk into the waiting room, "I'm walking one block farther to the East River and jumping in."

Dr. Ryan examines her and says she is now dilated to 3 centimeters.

We are jubilant.

"Hey," Suzanne says, "one more centimeter and we qualify for the birthing room."

"*What* birthing room?" says Ryan with contempt. "I never use the birthing room."

We are crestfallen. It has never occurred to us that the birthing room is too avant-garde and Southern California for conservative Dr. Ryan.

Dr. Ryan tell us it is still too early to go into the hospital.

"Have a milk shake and see a movie and come back here at 4:00," he says.

Suzanne is not comfortable sitting down for two hours, so we skip the movie, and instead go to a sort of health food restaurant near the jobsite called Au Natural. Suzanne is eager for lunch, although she is now restricted to a liquid diet, and I have still not had my breakfast.

I ask a waiter if Suzanne can have a special clear soup which is not on the menu, but he says no. I tell him Suzanne is in labor and isn't permitted to eat solids, but I realize Suzanne doesn't look remotely like she is in labor, and the waiter does not appear to be impressed. Suzanne orders a protein Athletic Shake and I have chicken Au Natural and a sidecar on the rocks.

The contractions continue, but Suzanne assures me they are not very painful. After eating we go walking the streets of midtown Manhattan, doing our Lamaze breathing every time a contraction begins, timing the contractions aloud, and wondering if passersby know what we are up to.

We return to Dr. Ryan's office at 4:00 P.M. for another examination. This time he says she's dilated to 4 centimeters, and we should go immediately to the hospital.

Is there time to go to Jeff's and get our stuff?

Just barely—he wants us to meet him at New York Hospital in twenty minutes.

Since it is now evening rush hour and a cab would probably take too long, we walk as quickly as we can the four blocks back to Jeff's apartment. We are beginning to get excited, but not frightened. Things are going too well to be scared, and, besides, we have had a dress rehearsal with the false labor.

Good friends of ours from Los Angeles, Kip Niven and Linda Lavin, are in town for tonight only, on their way to the Caribbean. We had made a date to see them for drinks at 5:00 P.M. We hurriedly call them to cancel, explaining that Suzanne is in labor and we are on our way to the hospital. Kip and Linda say they'll call us at the hospital after dinner to see how things are going.

Jeff and I and Suzanne and Jeff's doorman and Jeff's elevator man carry our bags down to the street and put them into a cab. Just as we are about to enter the taxi, we hear someone yell our names. We look up to see a woman leaning out of the crosstown bus. It is Shoshanna Ginzburg, wife of Ralph Ginzburg, who was my first editor at *Esquire* and the man who brought me to New York in 1962 to be managing editor of his new magazine, *Eros*—which is the reason I am in New York today. We have not seen the Ginzburgs in three or four years.

"What are you doing?" yells Shoshanna.

"Having a baby!" yells Suzanne.

"When?"

"Right now!"

Everybody crowds to the windows of the crosstown bus and gapes.

We get into the cab, wave gaily, and take off.

5:15 P.M. We enter the Admissions Office, where we had ended our hospital tour on January 4, and where the clerk had been too busy to issue us pre-registration forms.

There are no other patients waiting to be admitted, but the two admissions clerks are too busy to even look up. One is on the phone, one is riffling through a sheaf of papers. We tell them we would like to be admitted to the hospital, and they find this quite irritating. We persist, and point out that Suzanne is a maternity patient in labor.

They look at her for the first time and frown. Suzanne is wearing a full-length down coat which hides her belly, and an aluminum-foil crown with a tall green feather which her therapy group gave her at a pre-St. Patrick's Day party.

"You don't *look* like a maternity patient," one observes.

We ask them to trust us and grudgingly they check their records for the pre-registration forms we have sent in several weeks before. There is no record of our pre-registration. They check the computer. We are not in the computer either.

Suzanne shows them a xerox of her pre-registration forms and of the deposit we sent in. They mutter a lot and finally deign to admit us.

5:30 P.M. We have been taken to the Admissions Room on the main floor. In the Admissions Room there are four rolling hospital beds with curtains drawn around them.

A very nice young nurse named Vanessa tells Suzanne to get undressed, put on a hospital gown, give her a urine sample, and get into bed. I carry our bags over to the bed and sit down.

Vanessa attaches an exterior fetal monitor, which looks like a seatbelt with an extra-large buckle around Suzanne's belly. The extra-large buckle is a small transmitter, and the baby's heartbeat begins booming out of the speaker on the fetal monitor.

In addition to broadcasting the amplified fetal heartbeat, the monitor also emits electronic beeps in the same rhythm. Besides the auditory signals, there are also several visual ones. There is a small black screen with a fluctuating green fluorescent line. There is a digital readout of the fetal pulse which changes several times a second. There is a roll of calibrated paper which shows, in two parallel spiky zigzags, the fetal heartbeat relative to Suzanne's uterine contractions.

Vanessa explains that the fetal heartbeat should fluctuate

between 130 and 200 beats per minute. We both start watching the digital readout of the heartbeat, fearful it will drop below 130. It does. It drops as low as 73. We point this out to Vanessa, who says the fetal monitor may be shifting slightly on Suzanne's belly and is giving inaccurate readings. We are not greatly reassured.

A very nice female resident, Dr. Degann, examines Suzanne and tells her she is doing quite well. She says that Suzanne seems to be a lot more comfortable than many women who are dilated to 4 centimeters, and that Suzanne appears to have a high pain threshold. Suzanne's contractions are irregular, four to five minutes apart.

After a bit less than an hour in the Admissions Room, Dr. Degann tells us she has spoken to Dr. Ryan on the phone and he has indicated it is time to go up to the eighth floor labor rooms. We are still more excited than afraid, since things appear to be going so nicely.

Vanessa unplugs Suzanne from the fetal monitor, and rolls her bed out into the hall, with me close behind. Pushing Suzanne in the rolling bed, we enter the elevator. Operating the self-service elevator is a Hispanic gentleman in blue workclothes. Between the elevator operator, Vanessa, me, and Suzanne in her bed, the elevator is rather full.

Just as the doors are about to close, the phone in the elevator rings. The elevator operator answers the phone and calls to another Hispanic gentleman in soiled blue workclothes who is standing in the hall. The Hispanic gentleman in the soiled blue workclothes squeezes into the elevator with us, pulls the phone cord across Suzanne, who still wears her crown, leans over her, and commences yelling into the phone in Spanish.

The yelling continues. Suzanne looks less than comfortable, and the evidence indicates this is going to be a rather protracted conversation. Vanessa explains to the elevator operator the urgency of our trip to the eighth floor, so he closes the door and we ascend, with the Hispanic gentleman in the soiled blue workclothes continuing to lean across Suzanne's bed and scream into the phone. It is a recognizable New York Moment, and Suzanne and I exchange a smile.

We arrive on the eighth floor to find that the labor rooms are all full. We are taken to M-827, a tiny labor room which is never used because of how small and awful it is. It is less a room than a broom closet. There is scarcely space for Suzanne's rolling bed, but crammed into the room as well are a fetal monitor, a dented metal cupboard, a TV set on a battered extender arm, and a lazy-boy reclining chair upholstered in electric blue vinyl which is jammed stuck in the footrest-extended position.

There are no bathrooms on the eighth floor. If you want to go to the bathroom, you have to go to another floor, even if you are a doctor. Good planning.

Vanessa plugs Suzanne into the fetal monitor and the baby's heartbeat once more booms out, and the wavy green line and the digital printout and the spewing forth of calibrated paper resumes. To our great disappointment, Vanessa leaves. In her place we get a nurse with a thickish moustache, who is not nearly as friendly as Vanessa. She doesn't introduce herself, speak to us, or even look in our direction.

Suzanne and I continue our Stage I breathing, and I find myself transfixed by the fetal monitor. The digital readout continues to fluctuate between 130 and 200. I tell Suzanne how close I feel to her and how much I love her. She tells me she could never have done this without me. We hug and our eyes tear up.

The nurse with the thickish moustache is replaced by a fat nurse who also doesn't bother telling us her name and who doesn't appear exceptionally interested in the proceedings. She rolls in a chrome-plated IV stand, with an intravenous bottle of glucose water hanging from a hook.

A nervous young intern with the manual dexterity of an

orangutan squeezes into the room and attempts to insert the IV needle into a vein in Suzanne's left wrist. He jabs it in clumsily, and misses the vein by approximately a yard.

He leaves the first needle in her wrist and pokes about with a second one, as Suzanne grimaces in pain. New York Hospital has taken this occasion to have one of its slow learners practice on my wife.

The intern's forehead is beaded with sweat. Suzanne is biting down on her lip. My fists clench and unclench as I weigh the consequences to Suzanne's labor of choking the intern to death.

Finally, having stuck needles into every conceivable sector of Suzanne's wrist, the intern stumbles upon a vein. He attaches the intravenous tube, tapes it sloppily in place, and glucose water begins trickling into her system, providing nourishment and strength for her imminent ordeal.

Dr. Ryan arrives and gives Suzanne an internal examination. Her water has not yet broken, so Dr. Ryan reaches up inside of her with a plastic instrument and breaks it. The breaking of the water in this manner produces feelings of violation rather than euphoria, and when Dr. Ryan leaves the labor room, Suzanne begins to cry. It's not the physical pain, she tells me, it's the assaults upon her for the IV and the water-breaking that are so upsetting.

The nurse suggests we proceed to Phase II breathing and departs. I am breathing with Suzanne and trying not to watch the fetal monitor as it continues to register the fetal heartbeat and to beep in the way that we have come to know from doctor shows on TV. Suddenly, just like in doctor shows on TV, the fetal monitor stops beeping and sustains one continuous piercing tone. On doctor shows on TV this sound indicates that the patient has died.

The nurse has not returned. Panicked, I race out into the hall and shout for somebody to help us. A nurse rushes back into the labor room, takes one look at the fetal monitor and shakes her head.

"It's just out of paper," she says, and puts in a new roll. The nurse studies the monitor awhile, then orders Suzanne to roll onto her side in the middle of a contraction. The contractions are getting extremely painful. Suzanne is not anxious to shift to such an uncomfortable position in mid-contraction and asks the nurse if she can wait till the contraction is over. The nurse says no, and gives no explanation.

The nurse brings in Dr. Degann and Dr. Ryan and the three of them stand staring at the fetal monitor, conferring in whispers. I look over their shoulders. The baby's heart-beat is now dipping well below 130. It drops to 128, to 112, to 101, to 94, to 82, to 76, to 73. No one addresses either of us, and we are beginning to experience a terrible sense of dread.

Dr. Ryan says he doesn't think that the monitor is accurate, but orders an oxygen tank to be brought into the already ludicrously overcrowded room, and the oxygen mask to be kept over Suzanne's face except during contractions.

It is about 8:30. We have been doing the breathing, and Suzanne is now dilated to almost 5 centimeters. The contractions are getting unbearable. I try to imagine the pain and all I can come up with is that it must be like the worst and most painful bowel movement of one's life.

The doctors and nurses continue to hover about the monitor and whisper. No one actually says the words "cesarian" or "C-section," but everybody is thinking it.

Suzanne tells the nurse that if the last contraction, which was a killer, is as bad as it is going to get, she can make it without an epidural, but if the contractions are going to get worse, she can't.

The nurse confers briefly with another nurse.

"They'll get worse," says the nurse.

Suzanne has been trying to avoid an epidural. We've been told that not having an epidural is safer for the baby, and Suzanne personally feels more in control and in touch with reality and less panicky without drugs. But the contractions are hideously painful, and Suzanne is in agony over what to do.

I cannot bear her suffering. I cannot understand how women endure the pain of childbirth unanesthetized. I convince her to go for the epidural and we inform the nurse.

It's not that simple. First, says the nurse, you have to drain your entire IV bottle. How long will that take? Maybe twenty minutes. Then, says the nurse, the epidural takes ten to fifteen minutes to work. So it's going to be another half hour of excruciating pain till Suzanne can experience relief.

We have a new nurse. Her name is V.J., and at first I don't like her much. She has a loud nasal voice and she keeps calling Suzanne "Hon." I will grow to like her quite a bit in the next two hours.

I turn on the TV to distract Suzanne. I twist the dial, vainly trying to find something that will interest her, but the programs on now are substantially less exciting than even professional bowling. Before the IV bottle is drained, Dr. Ryan sends for the anesthetist to give her the epidural. The anesthetist arrives about 9:00, just as "Dallas," secretly one of Suzanne's favorite TV shows, begins.

The anesthetist is a pleasant young doctor of about thirty. He wears a green scrub outfit and a nametag which identifies him as Dr. Dinner. Dr. Dinner asks Suzanne if she understands what the epidural process entails. She says yes, sort of.

Dr. Dinner nods and begins to describe the process in great detail: First Suzanne will have to sit up and bend over, then Dr. Dinner will take a needle and insert it into the base of her spine. The insertion will take approximately ten minutes, during which time she is not to move or the needle will puncture her spine, which will cause a spinal tap, which will produce a rather painful headache for a day or so.

Suzanne says she had one of those and it was unbearable and lasted not a day or so but two weeks. She wonders how she can remain motionless if she is having a contraction. Dr.

Dinner says the nurse will help her. Dr. Dinner says spinal taps are rare—they occur in maybe 1 percent of all administrations of epidurals—but they do happen.

What seemed to be a sensitive doctor trying to allay our fears is actually something quite different—Suzanne is being read her Mirandas for malpractice in case anything goes wrong.

Dr. Dinner hands Suzanne a written release form to sign, absolving him of all responsibility. If she does not sign the release, it is clear that she will not get the epidural. She is in such agony I don't know how she is able to hold the pen and write, but she signs the release.

I am forced to wait behind a curtain in the tiny room as the epidural is administered. V.J. assists Dr. Dinner. I wince, listening as V.J. and Dr. Dinner caution Suzanne to remain motionless while the needle is injected, and as Suzanne warns that a contraction is beginning. I cannot imagine how Suzanne is going to be able to avoid a spinal tap.

On TV, Jenna Wade's murder trial has begun, and Bobby Ewing is forced to give damaging evidence against Jenna, the woman he loves and would have married, had not Jenna's nefarious ex-husband, Rinaldo Marquetta, kidnapped her on her way to the wedding, while Pam Ewing, Bobby's ex-wife, who is still in love with Bobby but who is also in love with her ex-fiancé Mark Grayson, who may have faked suicide in a private plane crash in order to spare Pam the awfulness of watching him die from his unnamed fatal illness, has just completed another wild-goose chase looking for Mark, this time in a clinic in Hong Kong, while J. R. Ewing, Bobby's evil brother, is trying to convince Mandy Winger, the former girlfriend of his arch rival, Cliff Barnes, to have an affair with him.

The epidural has been given, and I am permitted to rejoin Suzanne. In a few minutes the drug begins to take effect. She is still able to feel the contractions, especially on her right side, but they're much less painful. She is fully awake and alert. Miraculously, no spinal tap has occurred.

I begin to relax, and then I see that Dr. Ryan still looks worried about the fetal heartbeat. We ask if there is anything wrong, and everybody says no. V.J. is not permitting Suzanne to lie on her back at all, although that is the least uncomforta·ble position in which to experience a contraction. Instead Suzanne must lie on her left side. Suzanne asks if she can please lie on her back.

"*No*, hon," says V.J. with surprising force.

"Why not?" says Suzanne.

"Because," says V.J., "lying on your back is making the fetal heartbeat drop."

There is another whispered conference and then we are told that they are going to attach an *internal* fetal monitor. We know from Lamaze class that this is a bad development.

Dr. Ryan takes a length of insulated wire with a tiny corkscrew at the end of it and sticks it up inside Suzanne's vagina. From Lamaze class I know he is screwing the tiny corkscrew into the baby's scalp, and although I know it is a common procedure, I detest it.

The fetal monitor continues to give disturbingly low readings.

On TV, Ray Krebs, Bobby and J.R. Ewing's half-brother, has gotten drunk because his wife Donna has become more successful than he by striking oil, and she is pissed off at Ray because he has joined J.R. and Bobby in their fight to prevent Cliff Barnes and Jamie Ewing, a recently discovered cousin from Alaska, from taking over Ewing Oil by means of an even-more-recently-discovered contract between Cliff's, Jamie's, and J.R.'s and Bobby's dead fathers.

Is Suzanne following this? I believe she is getting at least the audio part.

The fetal monitor continues to give low readings, as Dr. Ryan and V.J. lean over Suzanne's belly, looking at it. Dr. Ryan is sleepy, having worked hard all day, and having just delivered somebody else's baby. The moon is full tonight, and Dr. Ryan will deliver many more babies than usual this weekend. (Rather more babies are born when the moon is full than at other times. It has something to do with the moon's gravitational pull being so much stronger when full, and with the tides, and with how our bodies have such a high percentage of water. But don't take *my* word for it, check this out with an obstetrician.)

As Dr. Ryan stands massaging Suzanne's belly and staring at the fetal monitor, he attempts to inject a little levity into the otherwise grim room. He tells of another time he stood in a labor room, sleepily massaging a woman's belly. He dozed off, he says, and a moment later the woman awakened him and informed him that he was massaging her breast.

"I was never so embarrassed in my entire life," says Dr. Ryan.

We both chuckled politely. I ask Dr. Ryan if he is worried about the fetal heartbeat. He says no. He is not convincing.

It is now 10:00 P.M. "Dallas" is over. The epidural has just about worn off. Suzanne is experiencing painful contractions again, but the contractions are beginning to slow down. There is a quick conference between Dr. Ryan and V.J. Suzanne is told that she cannot have anymore anesthetic because the epidural has slowed the contractions and there is danger to the fetus if it remains in there much longer.

A nurse comes in, addresses me as Mr. O'Malley, and says I am needed in the Admissions Office downstairs immediately. I ask why. She says she doesn't know, but it is urgent.

Numbly, I leave and go downstairs. I have a heavy sense of dread. I have begun to feel that the baby will die, and all I can think is how will we be able to bear looking at the baby clothes we bought in Paris or the baby equipment we bought at Ben's Babyland and Schacter's and Schneider's, and then it occurs to me that Suzanne could die as well, and the reason I am being summoned to the Admissions Office is to get me to sign forms so they can do a cesarian and so I will not sue them if the baby and Suzanne both die on the delivery table.

I go into the Admissions Office and say I am Mr. Green-burg, but they stare blankly at me, and so I say I am Mr. O'Malley, and this produces no greater shock of recognition than my previous identity. They don't know who I am or why I have come down there. I begin to leave, and suddenly they remember.

A middle-aged Hispanic woman takes me into an office cubicle and sits me down at a little desk next to a computer screen. I ask her if it's really necessary for me to be here now. She says it is. She turns on her computer and asks my name, Suzanne's name, our address and phone number, and a lot of critical data which she couldn't possibly have gotten by any means other than by yanking me downstairs at this precise moment. She says that Suzanne is not registered at the hospital.

I tell her how we have a xerox of our pre-registration forms and of the canceled check we sent in as a deposit, and she is suddenly able to boot up Suzanne's records on her computer screen. I ask how she is able to come up with Suzanne's records if Suzanne is not registered in the hospital, and I ask why I have to be doing this when Suzanne, whether she is registered in this hospital or not, is currently up in labor room M-827 in an emergency situation.

The woman finally takes pity on me and says it is all right for me to go—she will straighten out the problem somehow herself. I devoutly doubt this, but I keep my opinions to myself because I am grateful to be allowed to leave.

I start to go back upstairs, but terror of what I will find there makes me hesitate. I have more fantasies of disaster—a double funeral in the rain with a regular-sized coffin and a tiny one beside it. Selling the East Hampton house and the unfinished Manhattan apartment and moving away from New York to live like an embittered hermit.

I realize that it's been ten hours since I ate anything. I am not remotely hungry, but I know that unless I get something into my stomach I won't be much good to Suzanne or anybody else.

I search for the vending machine in the basement which I have heard dispenses yogurt. As I wend my way through the underground corridors of New York Hospital, I begin to pray and bargain with the Deity for Suzanne's and the baby's lives. I am now absolutely convinced that the baby will die. I am willing to settle for His just saving Suzanne. Somehow we will overcome this baby's death and one day even try again.

Going back up to the eighth floor labor room in the elevator, I hear a nurse say to the elevator operator, "They killed Morales's son." I do not know Morales, have no idea who Morales is, but I am suddenly desolated that they have killed his son.

I return to the labor room. Suzanne has dilated to 8 centimeters, which is promising—just two more centimeters and she will be fully dilated and able to start pushing the baby out. But she is having extremely severe contractions. V.J. has been coaching Suzanne's breathing, and Dr. Ryan has been massaging Suzanne's belly and staring fixedly at the fetal monitor for two hours now.

I try to take over from V.J. as breathing coach, while munching some trail mix, but the close proximity of my trail-mix-munching mouth to Suzanne's face causes her to announce she is going to throw up, and so I back away and defer to V.J.

V.J. works insistently and relentlessly with Suzanne on her breathing, and because it is a stranger and not a husband who is making her do it, Suzanne tries hard to comply.

Ryan examines Suzanne again and announces that she is finally fully dilated—10 centimeters! V.J. sprays Suzanne's vagina with iodine, draws Suzanne's knees up to her chest, and both she and Dr. Ryan insistently urge Suzanne to start pushing the baby out.

Suzanne pushes, and grimaces in pain. V.J. claims she can see the baby's head—a little patch of brown hair. Things start moving very rapidly.

"We've got to get this baby out of here!" says Dr. Ryan. He orders V.J. to get Suzanne ready for the delivery room, then swiftly takes me to change into a scrub suit.

Dr. Ryan leads me down the hall and into a tiny closet with shelves of freshly laundered scrub suits.

"Take off everything but your socks, shoes, and underwear, and change into these." Dr. Ryan then hands me a pair of baggy white pants with a drawstring and a baggy white short-sleeved shirt with a v-neck. "Oh, and don't leave any valuables behind, because they may be stolen."

"Tell me," I say, eager for reassurance, "is everything going to be all right?"

This man who has pooh-poohed our every fear during the pregnancy in an almost patronizing manner now looks at me a moment before replying.

"I'm very worried about the fetal heartbeat," he says.

It is not what I wanted to hear. A simple "Yes" would have sufficed.

I change out of my clothes and cram all of my valuables— keys, coins, paper money, credit cards, and ID—into the one pocket in the back of my scrub pants, wondering whether I need to be on the lookout for pickpockets in the delivery room.

I return to the labor room where Suzanne has been prepped for delivery, and V.J. hands me a goofy-looking paper shower-cap to wear on my head, a paper surgical mask to tie over my nose and mouth, and little paper booties to wear over my shoes. Suzanne gives me her rings for safe-keeping, which I squeeze onto my smallest fingers.

V.J. tells me to take along my camera and then she, too, warns me about leaving any valuables behind in the labor room. All this is tremendously reassuring. What you really want to be doing at a time like this is to be worrying about being robbed.

V.J. wheels Suzanne in her bed out into the hallway toward the delivery room, with me following.

"If you feel a contraction begin, hon," says V.J. to Suzanne, rolling the bed, "start to push, even if we're in the hallway."

The delivery room is ablaze with high-intensity lights. It looks a lot like a set for a TV doctor show, except this is real life. Suzanne's bed is wheeled up parallel to the delivery table and Suzanne is helped off the bed and onto the delivery table. It is not the most facile of exchanges.

Everybody is in green scrub suits and blue surgical gowns and masks and showercaps. Dr. Ryan and another doctor—possibly Degann, I can't tell with the mask on—move to a position between Suzanne's thighs. The high-intensity lights are trained on Suzanne's crotch. I am told to sit on a stool at Suzanne's right side and not to budge from there, no matter what happens. (I later learn they are afraid that I will faint into their work area—a common trick of husbands in delivery rooms.)

V.J. stands at Suzanne's left side. An anesthetist who is not Dr. Dinner is seated behind me. He will periodically, between pushes, place a clear plastic oxygen mask over Suzanne's nose and mouth. Three observers—either medical students or visitors from Ohio on a package tour—are standing behind Dr. Ryan.

V.J. and Dr. Ryan urge Suzanne to start pushing. Suzanne begins to push, and screams in pain. Dr. Ryan quietly tells her not to scream because screaming will neutralize the pushing.

I am half-paralyzed with terror, but I realize that, in the unlikely event everything comes out OK, we might want to have a record of this event. I force myself to raise Suzanne's Nikon from where it hangs around my neck and snap several photographs. It makes me feel a bit touristy and foolish to be taking pictures in such circumstances, but it helps to have something to concentrate upon besides the melodrama that is unfolding on all sides of me.

Dr. Ryan keeps urging Suzanne to push, and V.J. leans both

forearms on Suzanne's stomach to force the baby out. The pain of V.J.'s forearms on Suzanne's stomach causes Suzanne to scream again—a polite little scream this time, because Dr. Ryan has asked her not to scream and Suzanne is a very polite person—and Dr. Ryan once more tells her that screaming neutralizes the pushing.

Everybody looks extremely worried. Dr. Ryan tells Suzanne he is going to give her a needle of local anesthetic and then he swiftly does the episiotomy, slicing the perineum (the area between vagina and anus) to give the baby's head more room to pass through. It is nobody's favorite operation.

More painful and bloody pushing, and Suzanne actively represses the urge to scream.

"There's the head," Dr. Ryan suddenly announces.

The baby's head emerges from Suzanne's vagina, and then his shoulders, and then the rest of his body, and all at once I am looking down at a tiny baby, wet and streaked with blood and iodine, cradled in Ryan's hands.

This, the actual delivery, and not Stage III of labor, is the real Transition—transition from pregnancy to parenthood, transition from husbandhood to fatherhood, transition from OB patient back to GYN patient, transition from fetus to baby, transition from beloved parasite to actual separate breathing human being.

"It is 10:38 P.M." a nurse announces loudly for the record. Nobody announces "It's a boy," but it *is* a boy, and he seems to be all right. I do not cry as I'd expected and as I'd hoped. The delivery has been fast and bloody and terrifying, and I am much too drained to cry.

Suzanne asks to hold the baby, but Dr. Ryan says no, not yet, the erratic heartbeat during labor necessitates their doing some tests first.

Suzanne is instructed to push out the placenta, and I see it in the rectangular stainless steel pan they catch it in. The placenta is purple, veined, bloody, and ghastly looking, and I do not spend a lot of time looking at it. If people in California want to eat their placentas, that is up to them.

I go to the table where the nurses are washing off the baby. He begins to cry. They weigh him and test him and I look at him and know that this is one of the most important moments in my entire life and I feel tears about to spring to my eyes and then I feel them stop. There are no tears inside of me to shed.

"Count his fingers and toes," Suzanne calls to me.

I count them. He has the right number of each. Thank God. And he looks a good deal better than we were warned he would in Lamaze class. He is not blue, he is pink. His head is not cucumber-shaped, it is essentially round. There is hardly any of the cheesy white stuff called vernix on him that we were told might be there. He has dark hair, a lot of it. He is so tiny and so beautifully shaped and he is my son.

A nurse tells us the baby weighs 6 pounds 14 ounces. Suzanne asks her how long he is.

"The people who measure him don't come in till tomorrow," says the nurse. (Translation: "I don't do windows.")

Dr. Ryan starts sewing up the episiotomy. The baby continues to cry. A nurse swaddles him in a white flannel cloth and carries him over to Suzanne and places him on her chest. The baby stops crying. Amazing.

The operation is over. Dr. Degann congratulates Dr. Ryan on a difficult delivery. Dr. Ryan and everybody else congratulate us and leave the delivery room, except for V.J., whose job it is to remain and clean up Suzanne's crotch, which looks like a battle has been fought there.

We ask V.J. to take a picture of the three of us and she does. We are both in love with V.J. for the important help she gave us in the labor room and during the delivery. I would cheerfully have V.J. move in with us tomorrow if she wanted to. V.J. asks if Suzanne would like to use the birthing room as a recovery room, in repayment for the horrible labor room we were forced to have. Suzanne says yes.

V.J. wheels Suzanne's bed into the birthing room and leaves us alone with the baby for awhile.

Suzanne looks up at me, manages a weak smile, and holds up a single finger.

"What does that mean?" I ask.

"Just one," she murmurs.

"Just one what?"

"Just one baby," she whispers, grinning.

"You mean you aren't anxious to do all this another time?"

Suzanne just smiles.

We stare at the baby and hold hands, and we are still too much in shock to feel what we feel we should be feeling. We hug and kiss and profess our love.

Suzanne looks so pale and drained and spent. They have given her an industrial-sized sanitary belt that looks like a sumo wrestler's jockstrap.

V.J. comes to take the baby to the nursery and tells me to get our stuff out of the labor room, and I do.

Nothing has been stolen, but then I left nothing in the labor room worth stealing.

*

It is midnight. Suzanne suggests that I call Kip and Linda at their hotel—if they are still awake, I'll ask if they want to come to the hospital and chance that I might be able to sneak them in. V.J. returns to the birthing room and we ask whether we could sneak two dear friends into the hospital. V.J. says she doubts we could get away with it.

V.J. wheels Suzanne to the elevator and we descend to the sixth floor. As we emerge from the elevator, Kip and Linda magically appear. They have sneaked into the hospital and already seen the baby. We hug and kiss and we introduce V.J. to Linda, adding that she is the star of "Alice" on TV. V.J. does not seem overwhelmed—she says she already met Linda a few years ago while waiting for a plane with her kids.

We go to M-631, Suzanne's private room on the sixth floor. New York Hospital was incorporated in 1771. The rooms, it appears, were renovated in 1856. For $572 a day plus tax you get a grim, stark room with paint flaking off the high ceiling and a bathroom with no washcloths.

We take pictures with Linda and Kip and then they leave. Suzanne is famished and asks me to go out and find her a steak sandwich, a milk shake, and a large Coke with ice. I know she will never be able to eat all this, but I indulge her. It's 1:00 A.M., but there must be some place open on a Friday night in New York City.

I leave the hospital, trying to grasp the reality of fatherhood. It makes me feel proud. It makes me feel manly. Fatherhood. is manly. I have no idea what this means.

I decide to get some food at Rascals, a restaurant near the hospital which is a singles' hangout, but it's Friday night, and Rascals is so jammed that two dozen singles are standing in line outside, waiting to get in.

I once had something in common with these people, once shared singles' worries about getting dates and getting laid. Their concerns seem so superficial to me now. I push through the door of Rascals and a tough-looking bouncer asks what I want.

"I'm a new father," I say. "My wife just had a baby at New York Hospital, and I'm trying to get her something to eat."

The bouncer doesn't understand me at first. Indeed, I am speaking a foreign language here in Singles Land—the words "baby" and "father" have no equivalents in the native tongue. I repeat my request slowly, using hand signals and body language, and a glimmer of understanding animates the bouncer's features. He softens slightly, but tells me Rascals is currently too crowded to place an outgoing order. He recommends a place up the street, which is a 24-hour-we-never-close diner. But when I get to the 24-hour-we-never-close diner, it is closed.

The only other place in the neighborhood which appears to be open is something called The Jewel. I enter The Jewel and discover it to be a black nightclub. Four inebriated and well-dressed black gentlemen are scuffling with the maitre d', who appears eager to eject them.

When they have stopped scuffling, I tell the maitre d' what I seek, and once more it is as if I am speaking a foreign tongue. At length he tunes me in. He says his kitchen is closed, but the bartender overhears our conversation and recommends I try the Bagelworks, which is just down the street.

The Bagelworks is about to close too, although a Rube-Goldbergesque machine which occupies much of the left half of the store continues to spew out bagel after bagel and to send them off on a conveyor belt. I ask the young manager of the Bagelworks if he can sell me a steak sandwich, a milk shake, and a Coke.

The young manager is a tough New Yorker. He says it's too late, he's closing, besides which his slicing machine is broken and he can't prepare anything. But when I give him my new dad rap, he, too, softens, and comes up with, not a steak sandwich and a milk shake and a Coke, but a turkey melt, rice pudding, and a bottle of apple-and-boysenberry Snapple.

I return to the hospital with the food, and Suzanne, not surprisingly, can't finish more than a third of what I've brought her.

We talk about the delivery. We agree that the Lamaze breathing helped but that the descriptions of the pain of delivery were greatly understated, and the films of the births, with moms pushing out baby after baby with hardly more than a brow beaded with perspiration were a complete lie. The unruffled women of the films were either numb below the waist or had vaginas the circumference of the Holland Tunnel.

I tell Suzanne I was trying to imagine what the pain of childbirth was like, and I finally figured that it must be like the worst and most painful bowel movement of one's life. She nods.

"That's not it," she says.

We call Suzanne's parents in Dallas and her brother Jim in Denton, Texas. I call my sister Naomi in Sycamore, Illinois, and my mom who is vacationing in Palm Springs, California. My mother cries at the news of her grandson. I do not ask why she is crying. She is crying because my dad couldn't live to experience his son's son's birth. I call our friend Lee, who tells us today is the one-hundredth anniversary of Ring Lardner's birth.

Suzanne and I reflect about the labor and the pregnancy and how close we have felt during both. We hug and she becomes weepy and says she is sad that this private time of pregnancy is over.

I leave Suzanne's room at about 4:00 A.M. to go back to Jeff's apartment, feeling odd that my wife, my baby, and I each have to sleep in separate places. I press the elevator button, and when it arrives, I do not get into it.

I turn and go down the hall to the nursery. In the large brightly lit room are about twenty rolling metal carts with drawers. On top of each is a clear plastic basket with a newborn baby in it.

The babies are tightly swaddled in little white flannel blankets and placed on their sides. They are placed on their sides because their navels are too sore to place them on their stomachs, and if they were placed on their backs they could choke to death. They are swaddled because it is reassuring to newborns to be tightly bound—it feels like the womb to them. When they are unswaddled, newborn babies flail their limbs about because they have no coordination or control, which scares them because newborn babies don't know yet that their hands and feet belong to them.

The blue card in the back of Zack's clear plastic basket says "O'MALLEY BOY." I tap softly at the window and ask the nurse to see the O'Malley Boy. She wheels Zack's cart over to the window and resumes her work. I gaze down at him for a long time and wave after wave of emotion breaks over my head as I study him and try to grasp the concept of fatherhood.

I almost didn't choose to become a father. How awful that would have been. What is worse, I never would have known what it was I was missing. I would simply have cut myself off from one of the most exciting dimensions of human experience when I was already in the neighborhood—like being in Arizona and opting not to look at the Grand Canyon, or being in France and deciding not to see Paris.

I feel somehow that I have finally joined the human race. Become a part of history, if you will. There is no way to describe this feeling that is neither corny nor trite. There is also no way to express the notion that we have somehow stumbled into manufacturing a perfect miniature human being, with the correct number of ears and kidneys and toenails, without resorting to that hackneyed and overused word "miracle". And that this extraordinary little construction is also going to *resemble* us is almost more than any card-carrying narcissist's wettest dreams.

I must tell you that I am well pleased with most of the things I have written, either alone or with Suzanne, but this little job we have just completed is the finest work we will ever do.

Zack is sleeping, his tiny face going through about forty changes of expression per minute—frowns, grimaces, raised eyebrows, and little smiles that come from gas. From the movement of his little eyeballs under his closed lids, it is clear he is experiencing REM (rapid eye movement) sleep and dreaming.

Dreaming? Dreaming of what? What on earth could a baby only a few hours old be dreaming? How could I know what is in his consciousness, this baby who is afraid of his hands because he doesn't know what they are?

What do I know about this son of mine anyway? I know his date and time of birth, I know his weight but not his length, I know he has brown hair and blue eyes, I know that all his parts are there, and that is all I know. There are two strangers coming to live with us soon—one is a nanny from New Zealand, and one is my baby son.

When at last it is time to leave, I feel guilty. How can I simply walk away from the window where my own newborn son is sleeping, vulnerably displayed? It seems like such a callous rejection, and yet I cannot remain here looking at him and standing guard over him all night. I must get some sleep. I blow him a kiss and press the button again for the elevator.

✳

From the *New York Times*, March 9:

ALBANY, March 8—The wrong drug was injected into the spinal column of a pregnant 21-year-old woman at a hospital here, leaving her paralyzed and breathing only with the aid of a respirator, the hospital disclosed today. . . .

The mistake went undiscovered for an hour after the drug was injected, according to Dr. Gregory R. Harper, the attending physician in the case, who said he was not present when the resident gave the injection. By then, Dr. Harper said, the drug, vincristine, had destroyed the nerve cells along the spinal cord.

"It was the simplest of errors—misreading the label," Dr. Harper said.
. . .

✳

March 9. I wake up after only four hours sleep and try to fit back into the notion of fatherhood. It has lost a good deal of its reality. For the next few days I will notice that whenever Zack is not in the same room with me, I will lose the reality of his existence in my life.

On the way to the hospital I stop to buy five bouquets of red tulips and a silver mylar helium balloon with a stork and the words "New Arrival" on it. When the florist learns I am a new dad, she tosses in the helium balloon for free.

They have taken Suzanne off her IV this morning. She can now go to the bathroom instead of using a bedpan. She has also washed her hair and put on makeup and her own nightgown instead of the hospital's. She looks better, but she still looks weak.

Suzanne says Dr. Ryan came to see her this morning. He told her how worried he had been last night about the fetal heartbeat. He still doesn't know why it dipped so low.

The baby is brought in several times a day for Suzanne to nurse and for me to photograph. One time when I wasn't present Suzanne tells me an extremely grouchy nurse came to get Zack, snatched him from Suzanne and threw him in his bassinet so hard he bounced. I wish I had been there. I would've liked to make the nurse bounce too.

Zack hasn't quite figured out what to do with Suzanne's breast. It is, admittedly, a lot to figure out for one so young. Suzanne doesn't have any milk yet, but she does have colostrum, a clear fluid which contains a fair amount of nourishment and antibodies. Every so often, Zack's mouth and Suzanne's nipple collide and he manages to suck. And he is a very hard sucker. Suzanne points to a bruise on her left breast beside the nipple.

"Look," she says. "He gave me a hickey."

At the afternoon feeding, Suzanne is wearing her glasses when she puts Zack to her breast.

"Oh," she says apologetically, and removes her glasses. I flash her a quizzical look. "He doesn't like me to wear my glasses," she explains.

Seeing her nursing him and hearing her say this, I have my first realization that my wife and my son have a relationship apart from me.

Zack has dark downy hair that feels as soft as kitten's fur when I rub my nose in it, and there is a little whorl at the crown of his head. Where Dr. Ryan attached the internal monitor in his scalp there is only the faintest mark. I study the neat pattern of his coiffure and suddenly come to the curious realization that somebody has been combing my baby son's hair. As a matter of fact, it is the nurses who have been doing this, and the reason, apart from cosmetic considerations, is that they are stimulating his scalp to prevent an itchy and unsightly skin condition known as Cradle Cap.

Zack's feet are tiny, narrow, and wrinkled, the toenails impossibly small. His tiny hands have tapered fingers with minuscule fingernails that cannot be clipped yet, even though they should, because babies tend to scratch themselves. I kiss his microscopic hands and feet. They make my eyes water.

Suzanne changes his diaper and it is hard for me to look at his little umbilical cord with the tiny white plastic clamp at the end of it. It will be harder yet for me to look at his circumcision, I think, but we must arrange that soon, so it can heal before he leaves the hospital. The doctors, I have learned, call circumcisions "circs" and hate to do them—I guess they empathize too much with their patients.

I hold my baby tightly, recalling Bertha's advice that this is reassuring to him and reminds him of the womb, and I am careful to support his head because newborns cannot do that for themselves yet.

He looks up at my face with extreme interest. He is definitely studying me, trying to imagine who I might be. I have never been stared at in quite this way before.

My son is achingly beautiful, but at times he looks like a balding middle-aged man, like the cartoon character Mr. McGoo, like a Buddhist monk, like Yoda, the wise little creature from *Star Wars*.

When Zack fusses, I have discovered that tickling and stroking his head calms him down. I am aware that when Zack is a grown man of thirty-four, tickling and stroking his head will probably calm him down because of what I am doing now.

What a thought, that Zack will someday be thirty-four.

What a thought that he will someday be a teenager, disdaining me, holding himself aloof, asking me to borrow the family car. What a thought that he will someday even be able to talk. As all kids do, he will someday exclaim, "You don't own me!" You don't *own* me? What nonsense—of *course* I do.

All three of us are exhausted from the previous night. When a nurse has taken the baby to the nursery, I climb onto the bed with Suzanne and we fall asleep with our arms around each other. We are awakened by another nurse, one who weighs, conservatively, 300 pounds. She has brought juice. She looks disapprovingly at me in the bed and proclaims in a sing-song appropriate to three-year-olds:

"The *nur*-ser-y is for the *ba*-by. The *bed* is for the *mom*-my. The chair be-*side* the bed is for the *dad*-dy."

I glare balefully at her and don't move.

"Thank you," says Suzanne to her without smiling.

The 300-pound nurse finally takes the hint and lumbers out of the room.

I telephone a few friends and family members to tell them the news.

My friend Avery Corman, who has two sons himself, says: "I have only one piece of advice for you. Do not get a dog. You may fall in love with the whole Norman Rockwell fantasy of a boy and his dog romping in the fields, but resist. Do not get a dog. I speak as a dog owner."

I call my mom and my sister again, and learn that they tried to telephone us at the hospital and were told that we aren't registered.

When I reach my cousins, Eric and Carol Henry, who are expecting a baby in a couple of weeks, I unthinkingly begin telling them how tough the delivery was. Suzanne tugs at my arm.

"The delivery," I say, recovering quickly, "was a snap. Everything happened just the way they said it would in Lamaze."

*

From the *New York Times*, March 10:

MIAMI, March 9—When Bob East, a prize-winning Miami newspaper photographer, was wheeled into an operating room at Jackson Memorial Hospital eight days ago for surgery to remove a cancerous eye, he characteristically joked with the operating room staff.

Through a 33-year career with the Miami *Herald*, Mr. East was as well known for softspoken good humor and charm as for his wax-coated handlebar moustache.

An anesthetist put the 64-year-old Mr. East under. The surgical team went to work. Six hours later, with the operation nearing completion, a terrible error took place. A formaldehyde-like solution meant to receive and preserve the cancerous eye tissue was mistakenly injected into the patient.

The toxic fluid travelled quickly to the brain, causing irreversible damage. Mr. East was declared brain dead. . . .

The head of the team, Dr. James Ryan, appeared in television interviews to acknowledge that the episode was "preventable" and the result of "a tragic series of human errors". . . .

The question of medical accident has arisen in a lawsuit that received no public attention until Mr. East's death. Attorneys for the family of a 34-year-old Florida bookkeeper, contend that she was mistakenly injected with the wrong medicine during a tonsillectomy two years ago at a local hospital, leaving her in "a persistent vegetative state."

The National Center for Health Statistics in Bethesda, Md., reported that more than 2,000 patients a year die as a result of medical accidents. . . .

*

How much do you tip the obstetrician?

I know I agonize more than most folks about tipping, but this is a serious question. On our first visit to Dr. Ryan's office, he pointed out a painting that patients of his had given him after their child was born. They had gotten an artist in County Limerick, where Dr. Ryan grew up and where Suzanne's ancestors also came from, to paint his childhood home. It was, he said, so much more thoughtful a gift than the usual case of booze.

So a case of booze is out. But if he already has a painting of his childhood home in Ireland, then what is left for us to give him? Should we commission a painting of his office or of the eighth-floor delivery room in New York Hospital?

What would be a fair yardstick of how much to spend on a gift for him? Should it be 15 percent of the charges at the hospital? And what about Dr. Dinner, the anesthetist? Since he dispensed drugs for the labor, shouldn't he be tipped like a sommelier?

We buy Dr. Ryan an elegant clock from Tiffany's, and he appears quite pleased.

*

March 10. Zack has been circumcised. We had it done at the hospital by a doctor, not by a *moel*. I'm sure most *moels* are wonderful, but I have also heard horror stories about incompetent elderly *moels* who perform ritual circumcisions and who are neither clean nor accurate.

Everybody tells me that newborn baby boys have so few nerve endings in their little penises they hardly feel the surgery. I don't know. I hope they're right. Zack's penis doesn't look that small to me, and his scrotum is positively immense. I am told that this is normal.

When they bring Zack in for his first feeding after the circumcision, he is so sleepy he can't wake up. When we change his diaper I force myself to look at his little penis. It is wrapped in bloody cotton and it makes me shudder.

Suzanne's room is filling up with flowers. There is a basket of flowers and fruit from the Ginzburgs which arrived the morning after the baby was born, and it is as beautiful as any I have ever seen. When we call to thank Shoshanna Ginzburg, we ask how she knew what hospital we were going to.

"I stuck my head out of the bus window and watched which direction the cab turned," she replies.

Of course.

There are visiting hours twice a day, from 3:00 to 4:30, and from 6:30 to 8:00. A public address system reminiscent of the one on "Mash" orders all visitors out of the hospital at the end of visiting hours, then, five minutes later, orders fathers to pick up their babies at the nursery. Within another three minutes, fifteen or twenty white-gowned dads are trundling carts with babies down the corridors to the waiting moms.

When I prepare to leave the hospital about midnight, Suzanne gets weepy. She says she wants to slow everything down, to stop time. She does not want to leave the hospital and this special time of closeness we are experiencing here. She does not want Zack to get any bigger than he is right now.

I point out that, as wonderful as Zack is right now, there are other things coming up in his development which will be just as wonderful, or even more so—the day he shows he really knows who we are, the day he is able to hold his head up, the day he smiles a real smile and not one caused by gas, the day he learns to crawl, the day he first stands up by himself, the day he takes his first step, the day he says his first word, and so on.

She knows, she knows, but she still wants time to stop. She also wishes Dr. Ryan had positioned the mirror in the delivery room so that she could have watched the baby come out of her vagina—it would have made the experience more real to her, she says.

I ask whether she has doubts that the baby actually came out of her, whether she thinks, perhaps, that Dr. Ryan did a little sleight-of-hand and pulled Zack out of a drawer at the end of the delivery table and fobbed him off on us as our son.

No, no, that isn't it. I am, as usual, being logical and literal, and she is simply telling me how she feels. I suppose this is the beginning of post-partum depression. I spend awhile hugging her, and then I leave.

As has become my practice, I pass by the nursery and ask to

see the O'Malley Boy. They roll him up to the window, and I note that the swaddling is covering his mouth and partially obscuring his little nose.

I am certain that the nurses in the nursery know what they are doing, and I do not want to be the sort of parent I wrote about in *How to Be a Jewish Mother*, and yet . . .

And yet, what if Zack's swaddling really *is* blocking his breathing—would I really risk even the slightest possibility of his suffocating just because I was too embarrassed to ask a nurse to give him more room to breathe?

I tap on the glass. A nurse comes to the door.

"Listen," I say, "this is probably really stupid, but would you mind readjusting my son's blanket so that it isn't blocking his nose and mouth?"

The nurse gives me a thin smile, and goes to readjust Zack's blanket.

*

March 11, early morning. Suzanne telephones me at Jeff's apartment about 8:00 A.M., waking me out of a heavy sleep, with an urgent question:

"What's your blood type?"

"Uh, I don't know for sure," I reply. "The only time I remember being typed was in college in a biology class. Why do you ask?"

"Well," says Suzanne, "I told Dr. Smith, the pediatrician, that we were both type O, and he just came in very upset and said that the nurses in the nursery must have made some kind of mistake because Zack is type B positive, and that parents who are both type O cannot possibly have a baby who is anything but type O, so either you're not the father or I'm not the mother."

"Wait a minute, wait a minute," I say, sitting up in bed and trying to focus. "I'm not type O. Where did you get the idea I was type O?"

"You aren't type O? Then what are you?"

"I'm not sure," I say. "But I am definitely not type O."

"Why don't you call Dr. Baker?" she says.

Dr. Baker is our internist. I say I will call him and then I'll call her right back. I hang up and dial Dr. Baker's office. Dr. Baker is with a patient, but his nurse says she will look up my blood type in their records. She returns to say there is no record of my blood type.

"Dr. Baker has been my internist for twenty years," I say. "How could he not have my blood type in his records?"

The nurse goes to check again, and again assures me that there is no record of my blood type.

I hang up and call Suzanne, and tell her what the nurse told me.

"Wait a minute," says Suzanne, "it was Dr. Baker who gave us our blood tests so we could get married—he's *got* to have our blood types in his records."

I agree, hang up, and call back Dr. Baker's office.

"This is Dan Greenburg again," I say, aware how glad the nurse must be to have the opportunity of speaking to me again so soon. "It was Dr. Baker who gave us our blood tests so we could get married—he's *got* to have our blood types in his records."

Once again the nurse goes to check our records. Once again she assures me that what I seek does not exist within her files. There is a certain edginess in both our voices.

I hang up and call Suzanne again.

"There's nothing in Dr. Baker's records," I say. "But I know that I am not type O. In fact, now that I think of it, when we typed our blood in college in biology class, I think my blood type *was* B positive."

"You do?"

"Yes, I do."

She giggles.

"O.K. In that case, never mind," she says and hangs up the phone.

✳

March 11, late morning. I meet Suzanne at the hospital at 10:00 A.M. for a class in baby care. In the little third-floor classroom are eight moms in robes—two of them attached to IVs—and me.

The class is taught by a breezy, humorous nurse who does not give us her name. She tells us a lot of encouraging things about baby care, like:

"It's surprising how you can live on two hours of sleep a week." And: "Newborns have ten to twelve bowel movements a day. If you think you'll never do diapering and bathing as well as the nurses in the hospital do, remember that nurses do this eight hours a day, five days a week, but you'll be doing it *twenty-four* hours a day, *seven* days a week, so just think how good you're going to be soon."

She asks which one of us would like to offer our baby as a demonstrator for the bathing lesson. Neither Suzanne nor I is eager to have our baby used as a demonstrator. Neither is anybody else. Nobody volunteers.

"Well," says the nurse, "no baby, no demonstration, folks."

Finally a shortish woman with reddish hair and a Germanic accent volunteers her baby.

The nurse goes to the nursery and returns with a shortish baby with reddish hair and a Germanic accent whose name is Henry. The nurse unwraps Henry, who is not at all pleased to be unwrapped and begins to wail. Oblivious to Henry's wailing, the nurse proceeds to demonstrate how to bathe a newborn, punctuating every sentence with a "Right, Henry? Right."

Here are some things we learn as Henry wails:

You should shampoo and comb a baby's hair every day to prevent Cradle Cap. You can shampoo a baby's hair as often as three or four times a day, if necessary, because "babies don't get split ends or flyaway hair," but you shouldn't use soap on the baby's face. You should not bathe the baby in a tub or place him on his tummy to sleep until the umbilical cord falls off in ten to fourteen days. For the first two weeks babies have dry skin—"dishpan baby"—from the amniotic fluid. Circumcisions take one week to heal. You should bathe a baby "from the cleanest to the dirtiest, from the top of his head to his tush. With boys, don't take everything off him at once, because if you do, while you're cleaning the top half, the bottom half will pee in your face."

The nurse, much to Henry's and everybody else's relief, finally finishes the bath and rewraps Henry, then leaves us with a final thought:

"If your baby cries to be picked up, then pick him up. If you say he will then just cry all the time to be picked up, that's like saying don't eat when you feel hungry or you will then just want to eat all the time."

*

March 11, evening. I take a break from the hospital to do some errands—to visit the jobsite to pick up our mail and phone messages, to drop off at a photo lab the five rolls of film I have taken of Zack, and to go to the Lady Madonna Maternity Boutique to buy Suzanne another size 38D NeNe nursing bra. Not surprisingly, there are not many men in the Lady Madonna Maternity Boutique.

Tomorrow morning, March 12, we are leaving the hospital and going back home to East Hampton. It is a prospect that frightens both me and Suzanne. The nanny isn't due from Canada for a couple more days, and I think my own immediate terror is that we will not know how to take care of the baby or be able to keep him alive till the nanny comes. Suzanne's fear, as I understand it, covers a much longer time span than two days.

The only reason I do not share her fear is that I am so nervous about the logistics of the hospital checkout—how to get Suzanne, the baby, the enormous amount of luggage we've brought with us, and the staggeringly large number of floral arrangements we've been given out of the hospital and into our Jeep.

Our friend Lee has volunteered to help. I am interested to hear that severe thunderstorms are scheduled for our checkout. Well, why not? We came to New York in the rain, it is only proper that we depart in the rain as well.

Leaving the hospital at midnight, I find to my extreme displeasure that it has already started raining. I have left my umbrella at Jeff's, and there are no cabs, so I walk the four blocks back to the apartment in the rain, worrying that I will wake up with a sore throat and a cold, and that I will be forced to wear a surgical mask to protect the baby from germs.

*

March 12, early morning. I awake with a sore throat and a cold, and I am now forced to wear a surgical mask to protect the baby from germs.

It is raining hard as I go to the garage to pick up the Jeep, drop by Jeff's to load what luggage we'd been keeping there, go to pick up Lee, and drive to the hospital parking lot.

Judging by our experience with the Admissions Office, I am anticipating a good bit of trouble checking out. But there are not many people ahead of me in line, and when I step up to the window to pay my bill, I am told that the deposit of $687 which we sent in by mail should more than cover what our insurance doesn't.

I go upstairs to the sixth floor to get Suzanne and find that she is still nursing Zack, and that her milk, which had so far not arrived, has just now begun.

The arrival of the milk is called engorgement. Engorgement makes the breasts swell to the approximate size of basketballs, and makes their owner a tad cranky.

I get a handful of surgical masks from the nurse and put

one on while I am around the baby. Then Lee and I start packing up suitcases and flower arrangements and baby gear.

By means of a borrowed rolling cart and seven trips up and down in the elevator and lavish tips handed out to carhops and doormen, we manage to stow all luggage, flowers, balloons, babies, moms, and breasts into the Jeep in scarcely two-and-a-half hours. The process has been not as difficult as Stage III labor, but it has assuredly been more difficult than Stage I.

After dropping Lee off at his home and picking up sandwiches for the trip, we hit the Long Island Expressway. Hitting the L.I.E. makes Suzanne weepy again, and nostalgic about the experiences we had during the pregnancy.

"You know another thing that I'm nostalgic about?" she says, her voice quavering.

"What, hon?"

"I'm nostalgic about all those times on the L.I.E. when I couldn't last the whole trip without going to the bathroom. About keeping a roll of toilet paper in the glove compartment and having to pull over to the side of the road in the dark to take a pee off the side of the car."

I burst out laughing and she giggles through her tears.

Zack sleeps through the entire trip, strapped into his infant seat. He is still asleep two hours later when we pass Caldor's, a huge discount store in Bridgehampton, so we decide to stop off and buy a Swyngomatic and some Huggies. Suzanne goes into Caldor's while I wait in the car with Zack.

He awakes five minutes after Suzanne has entered the store and begins to cry. I put on my surgical mask, and am just about to grab a bottle and go into the back seat, when a car pulls up and parks next to ours, and the woman driving it turns to look at me. I do not know what she thinks I am doing in the parking lot of Caldor's wearing a surgical mask—preparing to go in and rob the store? Preparing to give myself an appendectomy? She backs nervously out of her car and scuttles away.

By the time we reach our driveway in East Hampton the sun is shining brightly, as if in honor of our arrival. We decide to mark the event with a photograph. Just as I am about to snap the picture, a UPS truck pulls into the driveway, and the driver gets out carrying presents for Zack.

"That a new one?" he asks, indicating the baby.

"We've just come back from the hospital this minute," I say.

The UPS man smiles a handsome, craggy smile, puts down his boxes, and takes a picture of the three of us in our doorway. If Norman Rockwell were alive today, he would have paid big money for the rights to paint this scene.

The cats are glad to see us back. They are puzzled by Zack. They come up carefully from behind and sniff him, trying to figure out what he is. It is clear he is not another animal. He is certainly not a person. They soon get bored and walk away.

"This is approximately the response they have to helium balloons," Suzanne observes.

Since there is no more danger of toxoplasmosis, I decide to let the cats go outside for the first time since the pregnancy began. They are extremely suspicious when I open the sliding glass door and invite them outside. They creep out, bellies low to the ground, and stay close to the house.

This is the day I change my first diaper. There's not much to it—you simply put the baby on his back, undress him below the waist, and slide the clean disposable diaper under his bottom before releasing the tapes of the one he's wearing. Then you slip off the wet one and tape up the dry one. The tapes of the dry one do not stick to the diaper as well as the tapes of the wet one stick to the baby's skin. You're supposed to cover his penis while you're doing all this, so he won't pee all over you, but I thrive on excitement and risk, and so, just like the great high-wire performers, I always work without a net.

Zack does not like having his diaper changed. He wriggles around and kicks his feet and cries. His legs are surprisingly strong, and it is all I can do to hold them between three fingers as I change him. The sight of his dried and shriveled umbilical cord is not as bad as the sight of his raw circumcision, and I am very nervous about touching either one of them.

Suzanne nurses him with her recently engorged breasts, but the flow of milk is still not enough to produce a steady stream. She has not really "let down" yet. That is to say, her milk flow has not really begun. Zack finds this both frustrating and infuriating.

As I watch this scene I am suddenly aware of something peculiar—Suzanne's engorged breast is bigger than the baby's head. As a matter of fact, the three globes—Suzanne's breasts and the baby's head—look like the three-ball sign outside a pawnshop.

*

March 13. Our first night alone with Zack, which started off so well, has turned into disaster. He wakes up at 1:00 A.M., and approximately every hour after that. Suzanne is up the entire night and is a wreck by morning, crying, fearful that she can't produce enough milk, that she can't take care of him, that she is stuck with an overwhelming burden forever.

I try to calm Suzanne down, and begin making urgent phone calls to find a baby nurse for the brief time till Karen arrives on Thursday.

"Don't be afraid because I'm crying," Suzanne says, trying to reassure me. "I'm just overwrought and deprived of sleep, but it's a temporary condition."

A dozen calls produce nothing but frustration, but our housewatcher, Sandy Jacobs, saves the day, managing to deliver an honest-to-God pediatric nurse from Southampton Hospital in our home within thirty minutes of my phoning her.

The pediatric nurse's name is Donna, and she will help us

with the baby this afternoon while Suzanne tries to catch a couple hours of sleep. If we cannot get anybody to do the late-night feeding, Donna says, she will stay here between midnight and four A.M. and do it herself.

Esther, our Colombian housekeeper from the city, arrives on the Long Island Railroad to help out too, and soon things are under control.

I take advantage of the lull to remove the Swyngomatic from its large cardboard box with the inaccurate illustration of it on the front, and, conscious of being about to become Dagwood Bumstead, I begin trying to put the thing together.

The Swyngomatic, I hasten to point out to any single or elderly or foreign person who may not know what it is, happens to be a small babyseat suspended from a superstructure which causes the seat to swing back and forth and lull to sleep whomever is inside of it. The device can be powered by either a windup key or a battery-driven motor. We bought the battery-driven model, partly because we were told that it is quieter than the windup model and will not wake the baby, and partly because it costs more and we generally like to pay as much as possible for everything we buy.

It is clear to me, after laying out all the parts of the Swyngomatic on the living room floor and examining the instructions in great detail, that the person who wrote the assembly instructions and the person who drew the individual parts and the person who did the illustration of the assembled mechanism never saw an actual Swyngomatic or had any contact with each other.

That I am not the first to note the poignant inadequacy of the instructions is attested to by the fact that one section of the instructions has been hastily rewritten, and a xeroxed sheet stapled over one of the printed pages.

To be fair about it, I must say that the assembly instructions were probably intended only for those who already knew how to put it together. The first draft of the instructions, however, was clearly written by the Marquis de Sade.

Two-and-a-half hours after I begin, the Swyngomatic stands assembled. I pop in the batteries and turn it on low. The babyseat begins swinging back and forth so violently it makes me dizzy to look at it. Well, if the baby doesn't like it, we can always use it as a punishment device: "You'd better behave, Zack, or we'll put you in the Swyngomatic."

Suzanne awakes from her nap and comes into the living room as I am standing, contemplating my handiwork. She looks at me and her eyes get misty.

"You're the dad not only in the good times, but also in the bad," she says, slipping her arms around me, "and you're perfect."

*

March 13, night. Donna goes home to feed her kids, then returns at midnight. Suzanne feeds the baby at 1:30 A.M., then gives him to Donna.

Donna will sleep in my office at the back of the house with Zack beside her in his bassinet. She will give him a bottle of formula and change him about 4:00 A.M. when he wakes up. Then she will wheel him into the kitchen and go back home.

Esther will stay in the guest bedroom and will clean and cook the following day before going back to New York on the train. And I will drive into the city and bring back the new nanny Karen in the evening. We go to bed, grateful that we will be able to sleep until perhaps 6:30 A.M.

I awake in the night and look at my watch. It is 4:30. I have not heard the baby cry, and I am a very light sleeper. Perhaps he slept a little longer than we expected. I doze off again.

I awake a little later and look at my watch again. It's a little after 5:00. Why have I not heard the baby cry? I know he cries when he wants to be fed, and I know he cries when he is being changed. Is it possible he is still asleep? How could that be? He awoke almost every hour the night before. Well, Donna is a professional baby nurse, and she certainly is on top of the situation. I doze off again.

The next time I awake I am shocked to see that it is 5:45. Is the baby still asleep, or is he dead? Suzanne stirs beside me and asks what's wrong.

"I'm worried about the baby," I say. "I haven't heard him cry."

"Don't worry," she says, "go back to sleep."

"I know I'm being a Jewish father," I say, "but I'm still worried."

"Don't give in to it," she says, and goes back to sleep.

I manage to fall asleep again for about twenty minutes, and then I again awake. This is ridiculous. It's after 6:00. Why haven't I heard the baby cry? Why haven't I heard Donna clunking around the house as she did all afternoon when Suzanne was trying to nap? If the baby *had* died, wouldn't Donna have awakened us? Perhaps she was so mortified she merely slipped away. No. The woman is a professional—if the baby had died, she would have told us. Ah, but what if they *both* died?

As quietly as possible, I get out of bed. If everything had gone according to plan, Donna would have fed and changed him and wheeled him into the kitchen before she left. I will check the kitchen first, although there is not the remotest possibility that he is in there. Then I will go to the back of the house and look into my office and brace myself for whatever is in there.

I tiptoe out of the bedroom. I tiptoe into the kitchen. To my utter amazement, Zack's bassinet is in the kitchen. I creep over to it and look inside. Zack is in the bassinet. I lean closer. He is breathing.

I cannot believe it. Donna did everything she was supposed to do, and she did it so quietly and efficiently I slept right through it. Donna is a real professional. And I am a real schmuck.

*

March 14, morning. We awake at 7:00 to the baby's crying, and Suzanne happily goes to feed him, refreshed from a night of sleep. I do not feel quite as refreshed as she does.

An hour later our housekeeper Esther comes to our door looking like death. She has awakened with the worst sore throat in the history of modern medicine, can barely talk, and is terrified that she has contaminated us all.

My God—the pediatrician had warned us not to expose the baby to anybody who was sick, to not even let anyone into the house for two weeks to see him, and suddenly what we have here is the Masque of the Red Death.

I snatch a surgical mask out of my nightstand, tie it around Esther's face and back her into the guest bedroom, telling her to stay in there until I can get showered and dressed and drive her to New York.

A short time later I am speeding toward the city in the Jeep. Esther is behind me in the back seat—her idea, so she won't breathe germs in my face. She is wearing a surgical mask— my idea, so she won't breathe germs in my face.

I have the windows open to permit the free circulation of polluted air, and I am freezing because, for some reason, the heater isn't working. I wonder if I, too, shouldn't be wearing a surgical mask. I wonder if it is such a good idea for Esther to be sitting in the back, right next to the infant seat. I drop her off at her apartment in Jackson Heights, Queens (a borough in New York), and air out the car.

*

March 14, evening. At 6:30 P.M. I pick up our new nanny, Karen, at the Barbizon Hotel. She arrived at 5:30 this morning on a bus from Canada. She has blue eyes and straight blond hair down to her waist. She has a strong New Zealand accent and is very soft-spoken, so at first I don't understand her too well and have to keep asking her to repeat things. She is dressed more like a skier than a nanny. She is lovely.

I am terribly anxious that Karen like New York and ask if she had any time to look around. She says when she arrived at the Port Authority Bus Terminal at 5:30 A.M. some disreputable-looking men made lewd remarks to her, and she was so upset that she went straight to her hotel and stayed there all day.

I tell her that the Port Authority Bus Terminal happens to be in one of the worst sections of New York and not to judge the city by that neighborhood. As we drive toward the Long Island Expressway I try to point out some famous landmarks on the Manhattan skyline, and I lose my way and have to stop three times at service stations to get back on the right route to Long Island.

Back at the house I introduce Karen to Suzanne and Zack, and we tell Karen all about the birth. Karen asks if New York Hospital has a good reputation, and we say the best. We turn on the 11:00 news and hear that a nurse was stabbed tonight just outside the eighth floor delivery room at New York Hospital where Zack was born.

*

March 15. Zack's umbilical cord fell off today. He also made his first poop since he's been out of the hospital. (Where does a baby whose diet consists only of milk get solid poop?) Dr. Smith had told us that Zack would either poop ten or twelve times a day or else be constipated for a week, and that both were normal. This is the sort of information I love, even if it's not true.

(When I was a little boy and couldn't sleep, my father told me to just lie quietly with my eyes closed and that would be as good as sleep. When I grew up I told him I've never had trouble sleeping because of what he'd said to me. He appeared chagrined and admitted that what he'd told me wasn't true, but I can still sleep anywhere and anytime because of it.)

Suzanne is upset that she isn't producing enough milk for Zack. She says if she were producing enough milk, her breasts would leak. Her breasts are not leaking.

I watch Zack sleep, watch his expressions change thirty times a minute. Interspersed with grimaces, raised eyebrows, and so forth are the fleetingest of smiles. I grab the Nikon and stand over the bassinet on smile patrol, trying to click off shots during the smiles' thousandth-of-a-second duration. We need a motor drive.

*

We are probably on safe ground with the infant if we begin with a few assumptions and work with the meager information that can be gained through direct observation. We see very little in the first two months that we can call "mental." In these early weeks the infant functions very largely on the basis of need and satisfaction. His hunger is ravenous hunger, the tensions it produces are intolerable, and the satisfaction of this hunger is imperative.

He operates on an instinctive basis, the mouth rooting for the nipple when hunger is intense, but not "recognizing" the bottle or breast on sight when it is presented. His inability to recognize objects at this stage tells us that the function of memory is not yet established.

If we can imagine this world or reconstruct it, we can only find analogies in the world of the dream. Dim objects swim into view, then recede and melt into nothingness. A human face hovers over him like a ghostly mask, then dissolves. Events in his life have no connections. Even the satisfaction of his hunger has not yet been connected with the face of his mother, not to mention the person of his mother.

—*The Magic Years*, Selma H. Fraiberg, pp. 35–36.

*

March 16. Karen is fantastic. Not only is she great with the baby, she also cooks and cleans and doesn't wait to be told to do things, she just goes ahead and does them. I have never seen anyone work so hard. I am hoping that she will like us and New York so much she will agree to stay a second year.

Having a stranger come to live with us is quite an adjustment, however. We no longer feel free to walk around partly dressed or to argue or even to talk about anything remotely sensitive or important when Karen is there. Indeed, Suzanne tells me she no longer feels our home is ours. The fact that Karen is an attractive young woman who frequently walks about our house in revealing sleepwear inspires brief fantasies in me which I am quick to quench, having long ago committed myself to serious monogamy.

Uncomfortable in the role of employers, we initially treat Karen as friend rather than employee, invite her to eat dinner with us, share confidences. It proves confusing to her and disruptive to the employer-employee relationship, and we are relieved when she herself chooses to eat her meals alone and to tell us less about her personal life.

This morning at 5:30 Karen brings Zack into our bedroom after feeding and changing him and puts him in his bassinet. But instead of going to sleep, he fusses and grunts and starts to cry. I get up three times to stroke his head and comfort him and replace his pacifier in his mouth. Three times he starts fussing the instant I am back in bed. So I finally bring him back to bed with me and put him on my chest.

I don't think you're supposed to sleep with your baby. I think it causes him to grow up and become a male nurse or something. I don't care. It is a very lovely feeling, and it seems to calm him down. He is not actually able to sleep, but he fusses only a little.

At 6:30 he begins to cry. I hand him to Suzanne for a feeding, but he doesn't appear to be interested in her breast. The instant she puts him on her chest he falls fast asleep. How do I feel about this? It is obvious that her presence is more reassuring to him than mine. It would be unnatural if it weren't, but it still makes me feel a little like a second banana.

Later in the morning, Suzanne gives Zack his first manicure. His nails are still too tiny to cut with a nail scissors, but he's started scratching his face and leaving marks, so Suzanne trims his nails with an emery board.

This is an important day for me. I realize today that it's been a full forty-eight hours since I've worried that Zack has stopped breathing. Progress.

The mail arrives, and in it a letter from New York Hospital:

Dear Ms. Suzanne O'Malley:
We are in receipt of the information that you recently sent us concerning your forthcoming admission to this hospital.

Upon contacting your insurance company(ies), we find that you do not have sufficient coverage for your forthcoming admission.

It is the policy of New York Hospital to request a deposit in the amount of $720.

A check payable to the New York Hospital should be sent to my attention prior to your admission. If there are any questions, please feel free to contact me.

Yours,
Mrs. B. Pabon, OBS Acct. Rep.

*

March 17, morning. St. Patrick's Day, the day that Zack was supposed to have been born.

We dress him in a little T-shirt and undershorts that are painted with big green shamrocks and we take several photographs.

It is both chilly and sunny. I decide that we should take Zack to the beach, if only for a minute. We bundle him up warmly, then Suzanne, Karen, and I put him in his babyseat and we drive to the beach.

It is an absolutely gorgeous day. Inexplicably, there are half a dozen horses on the sand as we get out of the Jeep. Everything looks slightly unreal. Neither Zack or Karen has seen the beach before.

I begin to worry that Zack is getting chilled. We get back

into the car and drive to Sedutto for ice cream—admittedly a curious choice for a possibly chilled child. We sit down at one of the little tables, and several people walk into the ice cream parlor and sit down next to us. I study them suspiciously.

"If I hear one sneeze from anybody," I say, "we're *out* of here."

Nobody sneezes, but I decide it's too dangerous to stay anyway. After all, Dr. Smith said not to expose Zack to strangers for his first two weeks, and he isn't yet two weeks old.

We return home and Zack cries to be fed.

"Nursing presents a whole new challenge in dressing," says Suzanne. "If you're not wearing something you can rip your tits out of in twenty seconds, you're in deep trouble." She opens up her blouse and unfastens the cup of her nursing bra. "Have tit, will travel," she says, exposing an enormous mammary. "Zack, this is the breast that devoured Cleveland."

Suzanne's milk is still not flowing as freely as it should, because Zack seems frustrated while sucking. Suzanne gazes fondly on his little face.

"I want to kiss him on the mouth," she says. "Look at those cheeks. I want to suck them."

As Suzanne nurses Zack, Wendell the cat jumps onto the bed and cuddles up between me and the baby and tries to nurse on my shirt. This is not terribly notable, since Wendell has been nursing on both of us since he was a tiny kitten.

Gladys jumps up on the bed and walks unconcernedly across me and Zack, then makes a nest for herself in the blanket at Suzanne's feet.

"Hi, Gladys," says Suzanne, "remember me? I used to be your mom. Now I'm just your owner."

*

March 17, evening. Suzanne is changing Zack's diaper. She calls to me in alarm. I come racing into the kitchen where she is changing him. She points.

"His belly button is bleeding," she says.

I don't love this news, but I also don't think it is a medical emergency. I dab at his navel with an alcohol wipe and say that ought to do it.

It's amazing. If somebody else is panicking, I am able to keep a level head every time.

That night I have my first sexy dream in several weeks. I dream that Suzanne and I are in a park and that I am extremely turned on by her. I tell her I want to make love, and she thinks it is still too early. We lie down behind a park bench and begin foreplay, and I am so eager I can't stand it.

I wake up and tell her the dream. We hold each other tightly in bed and we both regret that it really is still too early for sex. Six weeks is what they advise.

*

March 18, morning. Suzanne comes into my office in the morning with a beatific smile on her face.

"Guess what?" she says.

"What?"

"I'm leaking!"

"What?"

"My breasts," she says. "I finally have enough milk—I'm *leaking*."

She shows me the spots on her nightgown. I have not seen her look so happy in weeks.

"Congratulations," I say.

*

March 18, afternoon. Another trip to the A&P, another tabloid headline. From the March 26 edition of the *Sun*: "After Sperm Bank Mixup . . . GIRL GIVES BIRTH TO CHIMPANZEE!"

*

March 19. Suzanne is breast-feeding Zack on the other side of the bedroom.

"Zack, it's over *here*," she says. "I have a breast the size of Detroit and he can't find it."

After the feeding I am changing his diaper on the kitchen table. He suddenly pees over his left shoulder and hits the sliding glass door four yards away and the chair which holds a stack of his freshly laundered clothes. Yesterday he peed in his own face and scared the hell out of himself.

I bathe him for the first time by myself today. He is starting to hate being bathed slightly less than he did a couple of days ago. I am fascinated with his tiny body, and am still nervous about hurting him. As I sponge-bathe his bare chest, cover it to keep him warm, and then try to pull his teeny hands through the sleeves of his doll-sized T-shirt without snapping off his arms or fingers, I get sudden, almost subliminal, flashes of my mom and dad doing the identical things to me. And as this happens I come to know, in a way that hasn't been possible before, the love that they continuously lavished upon me throughout my childhood.

I mention this revelation on the phone to my mother later that night. It is too late to mention it to my father.

✻

March 20. My cousin Eric calls today to say that his wife Carol has just given birth. Like us, they were early. Like us, they had a boy. Like us, the delivery was tougher than they'd expected. Their baby was a half inch longer than ours, a half ounce lighter than ours. The similarities in our experiences seem overwhelming. I would rather talk on the phone to Eric or Carol about their baby than to anyone else about anything else. I am ceasing to be an interesting person.

I give Zack another bath and a manicure and pretend I am

Madge the manicurist on the TV commercial. He does not appear to be amused.

*

March 21. Today is the day I change my first poopy diaper. Zack hasn't pooped in three days, so there is quite a lot of it. Do not let anybody tell you that breast-fed babies' poop doesn't smell.

Zack screams bloody murder while I am cleaning him up, leading one to believe that he is philosophically opposed to being changed. Most of the mustardy poop appears to collect under his immense scrotum, which suggests that cleaning up little girls' diapers might be somewhat easier.

Changing poopy diapers is not the big deal that many people make it out to be. Two men whom I have admired immensely, my former college roommate and my own *father* (this is hard for me to believe, but my mother verifies it), categorically refused to change poopy diapers.

Make no mistake, there are many things I would rather do than change poopy diapers. But I would rather change poopy diapers than do many things.

For example, I would rather change a poopy diaper than put together my tax records for last year and make up a full year's diary of cabs taken to medical appointments. I would rather change a poopy diaper than have to watch somebody on public television urge me to phone in my contribution so they can tally it on the big board behind the bank of phones and achieve their intermission goal before they return to the show I was trying to watch. I would rather change a poopy diaper than read the pseudo-newsletter which accompanies my phone and electric bills every month, which pretends to be newsy and informative and which exists solely to convince me that their latest rate hike is justifiable rather than highway robbery.

I realize a curious thing today. Most of what I thought I was afraid of about fatherhood I am no longer afraid of. I am no longer afraid, for example, that I will be jealous of the attention that Suzanne is paying to the baby—I am definitely not afraid that she prefers the baby to me. I am no longer afraid that I am not grown up enough to be Zack's father—I truly feel that I am able to take care of him and his mother and myself.

I am a *little* less afraid that he will smother in his crib, and I check *much* less often at night with my penlight in his face to see if he is still breathing. I am still afraid that something will harm him—some disease, some household accident, some crazed motorist while we are wheeling him down the street.

Right now my biggest fear revolves about the infamous DPT (diphtheria-pertussis-tetanus) inoculation he will have to take when he is two months old. Sometimes babies have terrible reactions to this shot—death or severe brain damage. There have been some horrid news programs on TV featuring children who have become severely brain damaged from the DPT inoculation. I want a guarantee that this will not happen to my son.

*

March 22, morning. Zack is two weeks old today. Two weeks old. Zack's whole life so far has been the length of somebody's paid vacation.

"Zack is going to have to spend the rest of his life making it up to me for growing up," says Suzanne.

I think I understand that. The fact is, when Suzanne told me in the hospital that she didn't want Zack to get any bigger than he was right then, I thought she was merely being colorful. Now I don't know. I had never thought that newborn babies were cute. Now I think babies who are exactly Zack's age are the *only* babies who are cute. I recall an old song: "You have eyes of blue/I never cared for eyes of blue/But you have eyes of blue/And that's my weakness now." I look at older babies on the street and I think they are gross.

Suzanne is breast-feeding. Zack is not being co-operative.

"You can lead a baby to the bosom," Suzanne intones, "but you cannot make him suck. Zack, the other bosom has been waiting all *night* to feed you—if you don't take it, it will cry."

This is where it begins. The instillation of guilt in the child. The anthropomorphizing of inanimate objects. Suzanne is only half kidding. We have both grown up believing that inanimate objects have feelings. Intellectually, we know it is nonsense. Emotionally, we believe it. Our parents have done this to us. Our children are going to have it done to them as well.

Zack is fussy. Suzanne says it is because he is not getting enough milk out of her breasts. She is afraid he is not gaining weight. We are going to the pediatrician (I keep calling her the vet by mistake) in three days, so we will see.

I am not able to calm Zack's fussiness and crying by snuggling with him or carrying him around. I put him into the Swyngomatic for the first time, strap the seatbelt around him, and turn it on. The swing begins swinging back and forth. Zack is still crying. Then he realizes he is moving. He stops in mid-whimper. He looks surprised, then looks delighted. He closes his eyes. He goes to sleep.

Suzanne and I are mesmerized.

"That is really remarkable," I say.

"Yes," says Suzanne. "It makes me feel guilty, though."

"Why in God's name does it make you feel guilty?"

"I don't know. It's like putting him into a hypnotic trance. It's like giving him heroin."

I don't know. I used to think Jewish guilt was stronger than anyone's. Maybe Catholic guilt is stronger.

We watch him sleep. We are endlessly fascinated with his face.

"I just want to swallow him," says Suzanne, "which makes

sense, I suppose, considering where he was two weeks ago."

*

March 22, evening. Karen is going to give Zack a relief bottle of milk expressed from Suzanne's breasts and Suzanne and I are going to go out to dinner. It will be our first date since Zack was born.

Before we leave, Suzanne takes out the breast pump in order to store some milk for Karen to feed him. I watch uneasily as she attaches the clear plastic cylinder to her nipple, then withdraws the cylinder within the cylinder, thus sucking the thin off-white liquid out of her breast. I can't quite decide whether the operation is sexy and a turn-on or gross and a turn-off. It's probably both.

"I'm going to be slinging tit forever," Suzanne sighs.

We go out to eat at our favorite restaurant in East Hampton, the Laundry. It is high-ceilinged and very modern and softly lit, and the food is usually quite good. It used to be a real laundry. Many years ago, I used to take my shirts there.

We talk about the baby.

"It was yesterday I realized I was getting used to him," says Suzanne.

"How's that?" I say, recalling my own feelings of yesterday.

"Because," she says, "I looked up and I saw the bassinet, and for the first time I didn't panic. I don't mean that I was scared I didn't know how to take care of him . . ."

"Then what had you been scared of?" I say.

"His existence," she replies.

After dinner we go to the payphone and call Karen to see how Zack is getting along.

"Look," says Suzanne. "It's our first telephone call to a babysitter."

*

March 23. It is Karen's day off and we have decided to take

Zack along on our errands today. We buckle him into his infant seat and take him to the printer to order his baby announcements. Then we take him to an ice cream and sandwich parlor in Bridgehampton called the Candy Kitchen, where he begins to whimper. Suzanne whips out her breast and feeds him. I have seen other nursing mothers feed their babies in public. It is my impression that the other mothers did not whip out their entire breast in the process. If people are watching, Suzanne doesn't appear to care. In the past she has not always been this blasé.

Tonight I give Zack another bath. When I have gotten him all clean, I change his diaper. Just as I get his clean diaper underneath him, he begins to do a major poop. I wait until he is finished, then clean him up. I put a fresh diaper under his tush, and he begins another major poop. I begin to laugh. I wait for him to finish, then clean him up again and put yet another fresh diaper under his tush. He pees all over himself. I am overcome with helpless laughter. I don't know why I find it so funny. I suppose it is good that I am able to laugh at it.

*

March 24. Zack seems to have a lot of gas. He cried a good deal last night, and he has been crying off and on all day long. Nothing we do seems to give him any comfort, not snuggling him, not burping him, not feeding him, not rocking him in the rocking chair, not even swinging him in his Swyngomatic.

We are afraid he has the dreaded colic, wherein babies cry non-stop for the first two or three months. We have not yet met Zack's East Hampton pediatricians, Dr. Schonfeld or Dr. Quinn. It is Sunday, but we telephone the office, and Dr. Quinn calls us back immediately.

We tell him that we are afraid Zack has colic, hoping he will tell us otherwise. We tell him Zack's symptoms. Dr. Quinn says it sure sounds like colic to *him*.

"But he's been fine for the first two weeks," we protest.

"That's about when colic starts," says Dr. Quinn, "when they're two weeks old."

Our hearts sink.

"And how long does it last?"

"Two to three months. Usually it starts about the same time every day. He'll cry for an hour, and then he'll stop. The next day he may cry for two hours, the next day three hours, and so on up until about ten hours. That's about the worst it gets. After that it will work its way down again to nine, and then to eight, and so on."

The prospect of Zack screaming for ten straight hours is beginning to depress us beyond belief.

"Isn't there anything we can do for it?"

"Not really. You can try chamomile or fennel tea, but that's about it."

We thank the doctor and hang up. It is not a great moment. It is Sunday afternoon and it is cloudy and cold outside, and our pediatrician has just told us our son is going to scream and cry for two or three months for ten hours straight.

Suzanne goes into the bathroom to sob. I follow and try to soothe here. She is not going to be able to handle it, she says. When he cries for ten hours straight she is going to start to hate him, she says, and it will not be possible to keep him from knowing how she feels about him. She should never have become a mother, she says.

I sense that telling her having a baby was *her* idea, that I never wanted to be a father anyway, and that it is all her fault would probably not be the most effective way of consoling her. So I tell her that, even if Zack does have the colic, which I am not convinced he does, we will cope. We have Karen and we have each other. It will only be two or three months, and it may be a good deal less. I say a lot of other things, which I do not now remember, and their cumulative effect seems to help. She thanks me and stops crying and is able to leave the bathroom and go back into the kitchen with Karen and Zack.

Tonight I give Zack a bath on the kitchen counter, while Karen cooks spaghetti. As I change his diaper, I make lots of jokes about pooping, tell him it's all right to poop if he really has to, actually *invite* him to poop.

Zack doesn't poop. Instead, he pees across two sinks into a colander filled with freshly made spaghetti. Both Karen and I explode with laughter. Then we wash off the spaghetti and all three of us eat it for dinner. Either you love your baby or you don't.

*

March 25. Zack's first visit to the pediatrician.

We are seated in a large waiting room with several children and adults. A lady coughs in Zack's face. I glare at her, snatch Zack up and retreat to the other side of the room. I worry that the coughing lady's germs are even now slithering their way up Zack's little nasal passages and into his little trachea and on into his vulnerable little body—our friend Melanie once told us the only time her little boy ever got sick was following visits to the pediatrician.

An hour later we are called into the doctor's office. I undress Zack, trying not to worry that he could catch a chill, and the nice nurse puts him on the scale. He weighs 7 pounds 8 ounces. When he left the hospital he weighed 6 pounds 9 ounces—he has gained almost a pound in just under two weeks!

A pound doesn't sound like much, but it is one-seventh of Zack's total weight. It is hard to grasp the notion of anybody weighing seven pounds. A bowling ball weighs more than twice what our son weighs. Any of our cats weighs more than twice what our son weighs. Gaining a pound when you weigh seven pounds is like gaining twenty pounds when you weigh 140.

Suzanne is exultant. Never in recent history have I seen her so happy. She feels validated as a breast-feeder and as a mother. I expect this feeling to last at least an hour and a half.

Dr. Schonfeld comes in to examine him. She is short and cute, has dark waist-length in a braid, and wears a leotard and jeans. She looks roughly fifteen years old. She is very breezy and energetic, and doesn't seem to mind when Zack pees on her. She says he is a very healthy, very pretty baby, and that we have been doing a great job with him.

We tell her about our suspicion of colic. She says she doesn't believe in colic. She thinks newborns get so frustrated because they have no control over their bodies that they cry a lot, and the crying makes them take in air, and the air produces gas, and that makes them cry even more. She doesn't believe colic is either an illness or a problem.

"Besides," she says, "you already took him out of the showroom and now it's too late to trade him in, so you're stuck with him."

Dr. Schonfeld asks whether we have any more questions. Suzanne says no. I don't really have any questions either, but I have never been able to resist asking one when given the opportunity. I've noticed that Zack's right nostril appears to be slightly smaller than his left one and I wonder if it is big enough for him to breathe through.

Dr. Schonfeld looks at me a moment with genuine pity, then gives me a wan smile and bids us good day.

That night while Suzanne is nursing him, Zack gives her the first big smile of his life. Neither of us is willing to believe it came from gas.

*

March 26. Suzanne is taking a bath. Zack is crying, and I am having trouble soothing him. Suzanne suggests Zack might like to join her in the tub, so I remove his clothes and pass the baby.

While his navel was healing we'd been giving him only sponge-baths, so this will be the first real bath. At first he cries even harder at the unfamiliar sensation of warm water enveloping his body. Then the most amazed expression comes over his face—he appears to recall something quite similar and rather pleasant in his not-too-distant past, and he stops crying.

*

March 28. Suzanne has figured out why Zack has been crying so much lately. Karen has been giving him a relief bottle late at night to spare Suzanne the 3:00 or 4:00 A.M. feeding, and Zack has gotten spoiled. The rubber nipples flow more freely than the flesh ones. Not only that, but when you don't suck enough on the flesh ones, they flow even less freely. This makes Zack mad. He gives Suzanne a few half-hearted sucks, then bursts into frustrated and angry crying, and the first real tears he's been able to secrete in his life.

There is only one thing to do if Suzanne wants to continue breast-feeding—stop the relief bottles, keep him with us throughout the evening, and weather out his furious and tearful sucking.

We have a long night ahead of us.

*

March 29. Suzanne's nipples are sore from sucking. They are also cracked. The pediatrician and the breast-feeding books she's consulted advise exposing the nipples to the air to dry them out. Suzanne walks around the house all day fully dressed, but with her breasts exposed.

What do nursing mothers do who work in offices? Suzanne refers me to her current favorite book, *The Complete Book of Breastfeeding*, by Marvin S. Eiger, M.D., and Sally Wendkos Olds. On pp. 148–149 we read:

> Walk around the house with your nipples uncovered as much as possible. Get small tea strainers from the five and dime, remove the handles

and insert them in your bra to let air circulate around your nipples while you are dressed.

I don't know about you, but I would give a lot to know how many nursing mothers are walking around their places of employment these days with tea strainers stuck in their brassieres.

Come to think of it, though, bras with tea strainers in the cups are not much weirder than your average everyday nursing bra. A nursing bra, in case you haven't seen one, is just like a regular bra, except that the cups snap open and fold down to reveal the breasts. Nursing bras do not look like wholesome articles of clothing which are appropriate for serious nursing mothers. They look like mail-order items from a Frederick's of Hollywood catalogue, in the same tradition as nippleless bras and crotchless panties.

*

March 30. Zack is still furious at the inefficiency of human nipples. It's going to be another long night. To preserve Suzanne's sanity, we are going out to dinner before the fun begins back home. Before we leave, Suzanne gives Zack his dinner.

"Hi, Zack," she says, unsnapping the lewd cups of her nursing bra. "It's me, the cow."

Once seated at the restaurant, it occurs to both of us to phone Karen and give her the number where we are dining. I call our home. There is no answer. I call again. I let it ring thirty times. There is still no answer.

I think I know what has happened. Karen is in her room at the other end of the house and cannot hear the phone ring. It is either that, or fire has whooshed through the house in the brief time we've been gone and incinerated them both.

I have not been in therapy so many years for nothing. I know that there has been no fire. I know Karen simply cannot hear the phone. I do not get into the car and tear back home. I go back to the table and eat a leisurely dinner and congratulate myself on my mental health.

After dinner I drive with deliberate slowness back to our house. There is no telltale orangey glow in the sky. The house is intact. Zack is in his bassinet. Karen is in her room. Karen is surprised to hear that I telephoned. She did not hear the phone ring. I am so proud I did not panic.

I go into my office and work till 3:00 A.M. (It is important to point out here that Zack's arrival has not forced me to stop working—tempting as it is to make you think I am the primary caretaker, Karen and Suzanne spend more time with him than I do.) When I finally come to bed, Suzanne informs me that Zack has been crying for the past two hours. As my head touches the pillow he begins again. Will I please take him into the kitchen and rock him in the rocking chair? I will.

I pick him up. I take him into the kitchen. I sit down in the rocking chair. He is still crying. The crying has scared him and made him hysterical. The sound of a newborn's hysterical crying that close to your ears, especially at that hour of the night, is particularly grating.

It is also a rebuke, a rejection, a refutation of everything that you believe or aspire to about your present and future relation to that baby and of your ultimate worth in nurturing and comforting him. I do not for a moment condone the hideous things that demented parents do to babies when they reach the end of their tether and their reason, but I cannot tell you that I don't understand a little bit about what motivates them.

I hold Zack against my chest with my face against his and begin rocking him back and forth and speaking to him in a reasonable manner. I find him not totally unreasonable. By 3:20 A.M. he is no longer screaming but crying. By 3:30 he is not crying but whimpering. By 3:40 he is not whimpering but lightly dozing. By 3:50 he is deeply asleep. I am terribly proud of my soothing and sleep-inducing abilities. I feel my fatherhood once more re-validated.

I tiptoe into our bathroom where his bassinet has been wheeled, and I gently put him down on his stomach. Zack's navel is by now completely healed, and most babies love to sleep on their stomachs. The only problem is, when a baby sleeps on his stomach, his nose and mouth could become obstructed and he could suffocate. This is not what I have been told by nurses or doctors, this is just common sense.

I watch Zack sleep on his stomach. He is very calm. He is a bit *too* calm. I lean down next to him to see if I can hear him breathing. I can just barely make out a very light breath.

I take out my penlight and shine it on his head. Just as I'd suspected, he's lying on his face and his little nose and mouth are partly obstructed by the bed. I try to turn his head to one side easily and, as nervous as I am about his suffocating, I am also a little nervous about twisting his neck too hard and breaking it.

I stand up. This is foolish. It is now well past 4:00 A.M. He will be up and crying to be fed again in about two hours. Assuming he doesn't suffocate, that is.

I lean down again and listen. I can hardly hear him breathe. I do not want to be the Shirley MacLaine character in *Terms of Endearment* who climbs into her baby's crib because she fears it has stopped breathing. I also don't want to be the father of a dead baby. I give him a little push. He responds with the faintest of grunts. At least I *think* he has grunted. What if he hasn't? What if it is my imagination? What if he has already stopped breathing?

I give him a little harder push. He responds with a slightly more audible grunt. OK, Dan, isn't that enough for you? It should be, it really should be. And it *would* be, were it not well after 4:00 A.M. and were I not exhausted beyond reason. But it *is* well after 4:00 A.M., and I *am* exhausted beyond reason, and I have suddenly begun to imagine that he is actually unable to breathe and that what I heard was not a healthy sleepy grunt but a tiny baby death rattle, and what therapy

gains in restaurants while phoning sitters early in the evening it loses over bassinets in bathrooms at the hour of the wolf.
I push him again, and he starts to cry.
Thank God.

*

April 4. The pediatrician has given us some literature. At the top it says: "IMPORTANT INFORMATION ABOUT DIPHTHERIA, TETANUS, AND PERTUSSIS AND DTP, DT, AND TD VACCINES. Please read this carefully."
I read it carefully. Table 9 is entitled "Side Effects and Adverse Reactions Occurring Within 48 Hours of Pertussis Immunizations" and lists: Redness at site, Swelling at site, Pain at site, Fever, Drowsiness, Fretfulness, Anorexia, Vomiting, Persistent crying (3 to 21 hour duration), High-pitched unusual cry, Convulsions, Collapse with shock-like state."

*

April 5. The cats may *say* they aren't affected by Zack's presence in our household, but I don't believe them. Gladys climbs up on Zack's changing table and sleeps on it whenever it's not in use, and Wendell now sleeps only in Zack's bassinet or in his pram.

*

April 7. Easter Sunday. After Easter services and Easter dinner we return home and begin to shoot a videotape of Zack. Zack will look at this tape years from now when he is grown and videotapes will seem as quaint to him as the 8 mm. black-and-white movies that my dad made of me seem today.
I recently had several of my dad's 8 mm. films transferred to a videotape cassette, and once again marveled at the creativity and care he exhibited when making them. Each sequence is introduced by beautifully lettered and humorously illustrated cards, because my dad was an artist and a very funny man.

There is one film called "Sunday in the Park." It shows me and my dad getting ready to go to the park. It shows my mom talking on the phone—still a favorite activity of hers. It shows me and my dad waiting patiently for Mom to conclude her phone conservation. There are shots of a clock with advancing hands, a calendar with shedding leaves, and Mom continues to talk on the phone. I play outside in my sunsuit, then I'm in my snowsuit, building a snowman, and Mom continues to talk on the phone. Dad's face grows a bushy black beard, which turns gray, then white, and Mom continues to talk on the phone.

We don't have the patience to spend that kind of time making our videotapes of Zack. I hope he will forgive us when he grows up.

Zack is remarkably well-behaved during the shooting, but when it concludes he begins to cry.

I am told that Eskimos have several words for snow. I can now identify as many varieties of Zack's crying as the Eskimos have words for snow.

For example, there is one which goes: "Uh-huh uh-huh uh-huh uh-huh uh-huh . . ." There is one which goes: "Gyaaaahh! Gyaaaahh! Gyaaaahh! Gyaaaahh! Gyaaaahh!" There is one which goes: "Uh-WAH! Uh-WAH! Uh-WAH! Uh-WAH! Uh-WAH!" There is one which goes: "Uh-huh uh-huh uh-huh WAAAAAAAAAAAAAAAAAAAAAAAAAAAAAAAAAA-AAAAAAAAAAAAAAHHHHHHHHHHHHH!" There is one which sounds like stepping on a cat's tail for a prolonged period of time, although stepping on a cat's tail for a prolonged period of time is much the pleasanter sound.

When Zack cries I carry him around the room. The faster I walk and the more I jiggle him while walking, the less he cries. Only vigorous bouncing seems to comfort him (is this the derivation of the term "bouncing baby boy"?). The harder I bounce him, the better he seems to like it. His tiny eyes grow so wide they're almost popping, his tiny face is blurring in and out of my laser-like focus with every bounce. It might look to the uninformed observer as though I am mistreating him, and yet, if I bounce him more slowly or less violently he resumes his frenzied crying.

What is it about the bouncing that he likes? Surely it isn't that it reminds him of what it felt like in the womb—Suzanne didn't bound around like a crazed kangaroo when she was pregnant. Perhaps the bouncing moves the gas through his digestive system toward either aperture and relieves his cramps. Perhaps the bouncing is violent enough to wholly claim his attention and get it off his pain.

Eventually, his popping eyes no longer pop. The lids begin, ever so slowly, to come together. It is absurd that such strenuous bouncing could induce sleep, and yet that is what appears to be happening. But every time his eyes are closed for more than a minute and I decrease the severity of my bouncing, the lids snap open again and he begins to cry. And so I step up the bouncing, and once more the eyes begin to close, and when I am certain that he is asleep I stop the bouncing and he bursts into angry tears.

After an hour and a half of such sleep-teasing, I am demoralized. Reaching out for sleep, coming so close to it, and having it snatched away again is a particularly insidious kind of torture.

"You're killing me, Zack," I say in frustration. "You are killing your father!"

Suzanne looks at me in alarm.

*

April 8. Zack is one month old today. Today is also Suzanne's birthday.

Suzanne is depressed because last night I told Zack he was killing me. Suzanne takes the melodramatic things I say quite literally. She retaliates for my pronouncement by informing me that she is having the worst birthday of her life.

Tonight I give Suzanne two flowering plants, a bunch of helium balloons, a fluorescent magenta sweatshirt, a yellow baseball cap, and an album containing 5 × 7 blowups of the photographs I shot of her and Zack in the delivery room. Then we go to dinner at the only good French restaurant in East Hampton, which we have completely to ourselves because it is Monday night in the off-season, and she admits that she isn't having the worst birthday of her life after all.

But as nice as the evening is, the high point of Suzanne's day came earlier—just before 5:00 P.M. we were at the post office, where Suzanne beheld a woman in her eighth or ninth month of pregnancy. Suzanne took one look at the woman and began to cackle in a manner so evil that it chilled my blood.

*

April 13. We do not understand why pediatricians insist they do not know what colic is or what causes it. It is clear to us that colic is caused by gas pains. We can see the direct relationship between Zack's grimaces and cries of pain and the bubbles of gas we feel gurgling through his little body, between his burps and farts and the consequent relief of his pain. We do not understand what pediatricians do not understand.

As bad as colic is, we have been assured by every pediatrician we've talked to that it is not an illness and that it will pass when he is eight weeks old. Except that today I hear a term that strikes terror into my heart. The term is Six-Month Colic.

Zack's fingers and hands are constantly in motion, like sea anemones. He is beginning to gain control of his movements. He is beginning to be able to hold his head upright instead of flopping over to the side. When he is held in an upright burping position he now sometimes throws himself into a horizontal cuddling position, because he likes cuddling better than burping. If you return an object to his field of vision within two-and-a-half seconds, he remembers it.

Suzanne has been teaching Zack to smile. She lightly touches his chin and nose and cheeks and coaxes him, smiles at him herself, and this sometimes produces a lovely toothless grin on his face. How did she know how to do this? More important, how did he?

*

April 15. Newborn babies have a curious effect on people. The gruffest cab drivers and waitresses and tradespeople get absolutely mushy in the presence of newborn babies.

And everybody gives you advice—the most contradictory, the most patently worthless advice I have ever heard, has been given to me about my baby, and I do not ever recall asking anybody for it. We sent our housekeeper, Esther, to a four-session course in babycare given by the Red Cross at the 92nd Street Y, and as our reward we now get to hear from her all the things we are doing wrong.

For example, Esther (who, by the way, has never had children of her own) recently informed me that the diaper wipes we are using will dry out the baby's skin and should be thrown away, that it is not necessary to speak quietly when the baby is sleeping because he must learn to live in a household with normal noises, and that we must not pick the baby up every time he cries or he will cry to be picked up all the time. A little knowledge is a dangerous thing.

Our birth announcement features a photograph I took of Zack in the delivery room about three seconds after his birth. The doctor is holding him in his hands. The umbilical cord is visible, and there is a little of what appears to be blood but which is actually iodine on the baby's face. The doctor is withdrawing liquids from the baby's mouth with a rubber bulb.

It is, in all humility, an extraordinary photograph, and it is also a little shocking. It is not a picture of a cleaned-up baby with a little pink bow. It is a real baby which just came out of a real mother and it is a little too much reality for most people who have seen it, I think. Most people who have gotten the birth announcement have told me it was "interesting" or "unusual." My mother expresses cautious enthusiasm for our birth announcement on the phone tonight.

"My only worry," she says, "is whether Zack will like it when he grows up."

*

April 16. Both Suzanne and I have been excused from jury service on several previous occasions by letter. We have both been called again, and must now appear in person to be excused. We have been told that we are eligible to be excused permanently if we can prove we are the sole proprietors of our business—which, in fact, we are. We assemble recent tax returns and copies of our books and videotapes of our movies and we drive into New York with the baby and sit in a crowded waiting room in the courthouse, waiting to be called by the examiner.

Zack is unusually cranky and begins to scream. His face gets very red, his mouth so large and round it looks like cartoons of crying babies. Nobody in the waiting room looks directly at us, but the tension is so great that if I touched any one of them lightly on the arm I believe they would literally explode, little pieces spraying all over the walls. No longer able to take it, the receptionist pushes us into the examiner's office ahead of everybody else—perhaps the only advantage of owning a colicky baby.

We are not quite so lucky with the examiner, a woman with a definite attitude. As Zack wails, she informs us that we cannot be excused from jury service, even though we are the sole proprietors of our own business, because movie studios withhold taxes from our screenwriting fees, and anyone who has taxes withheld from his pay is not considered to be the sole proprietor of his business.

Suzanne, however, can be excused as a mother, provided

she changes her classification from full-time to part-time writer on her application. Suzanne feels this to be sexist and demeaning, but she is not eager to breast-feed Zack in the jury box, so she makes the change.

In the lobby Zack is found to have severe diarrhea. He has pooped through his diaper and his yellow cotton pants and gotten it all over everything in sight. Further, he has somehow gotten a firm grip on his hair and, unaware that it is his, he is pulling it and screaming from the pain.

I shall not burden you with further details of our activities on this day; I shall merely mention a medical expression we learned as a result of it. The medical expression is "projectile diarrhea."

Driving back to East Hampton on the L.I.E., Zack falls asleep. Suzanne had taken the baby to show the members of her therapy group before tonight's session began.

Suzanne is the only member of her group who is currently married and the only woman in her group who has a child. She says some members of her group are upset that they have no prospects of having children before their biological clocks run out. Suzanne told them she's glad she has a child, but she wouldn't be a lesser person if she weren't a mother.

I tell her I don't think children are for everyone, and I never thought they were for me, but I do now. I tell her that, as tough as today and the past several days have been, if a magical person appeared and took me back in time to the period just before we conceived, I would still choose to have this baby. What we go through with him is an adventure which we are both experiencing mutually and which is drawing us closer and closer together. And with the luxury of having Zack finally asleep in his infant seat, I am able to see the humor in the events just concluded and to almost be nostalgic about them. (Perhaps the nostalgia part is going too far to make a point.)

It is close to 9:00 P.M. as we leave the L.I.E. at Exit 70 and pass by the Gateway Diner. Although we are both quite hungry, we cannot bear the idea of inflicting a screaming baby on these good people again. Indeed, I have the impression that, were we to walk up to their door with little Zack in our arms, they would behave like the saloonkeepers did in old Westerns when the villains rode into town, hastily shuttering the bar and pretending to be closed.

We go instead to another old haunt of the pregnancy, the Holiday Diner in Southampton, where we have never been with Zack. The waitress remembers Suzanne as the lady with the large belly who used to come there once a week, and coos over the still sleeping baby. By the time food comes Zack awakes and the crying commences.

I change his diarrhetic diaper on the seat of our booth, and we both wolf down our food and beat a hasty retreat to the car.

He screams when we get him home. I change another poopy diaper, give him a bath, and do High-Stepping Horses with him till he falls asleep and I can permit myself the luxury of falling unconscious on the bed.

On many occasions before the pregnancy Suzanne had expressed grave doubts that I would help out with the baby—doubts which, incidentally, I had thought quite reasonable. Now she looks at me fondly in my zombie-like state on the bed and says:

"You really know how to take care of your son—you change his poopy diapers, you bathe him, you work through his screaming and calm him down and put him to sleep. You're a real participating father."

I am so damned proud.

*

April 18. Getting out of bed this morning for the dawn feeding, Karen sleepily picked Zack up out of his bassinet, then got her legs tangled up in her own sheets and began to fall. In the process she gripped Zack's body so tightly that she left bruises on it, but, thankfully, she didn't drop him.

I take the Hampton Jitney into New York for the day by myself. On the way back I notice that there is a newborn in the seat ahead of mine. It is a boy, and he is totally bald, but I tell his mother he is cute. I ask her how old he is. Four weeks, she says. I tell her I have a baby who is five-and-a-half weeks.

"Good," she says. "Then you won't mind it when my son cries all the way to the Hamptons."

But her baby doesn't cry at all on the way to the Hamptons. Not one sound from him throughout the entire trip. On the other hand, he is bald.

*

April 19, late evening. Suzanne's cousin Nancy O'Malley calls to congratulate us and find out how the baby is doing. She tells us she and her husband are contemplating having a child. Suzanne proceeds to tell her how painful the delivery was and how much Zack cries now.

When we get off the phone, Suzanne has the same evil gleam in her eye I saw the day of her birthday when she spied the pregnant woman at the post office. I think Suzanne is going to enjoy frightening expectant mothers.

*

April 20, evening. I have been eating dinner with one hand, and rocking and bouncing Zack to sleep with the other. His eyes are now closed. I very carefully stand up and carry him to his bassinet and put him down on his belly. I have invested about two hours in this sleep-induction process so far. If I haven't waited long enough, or if I've waited too long to put him down, then I have blown two hours and get to start all over again.

I watch him anxiously in his bassinet. He moves and whimpers. It might be an isolated whimper, or it might be the start of earnest crying. If it's an isolated whimper, I mustn't pick him up—I must either pat him gently on the back or not touch him at all and he will continue sleeping. If it's the start of earnest crying, I must pick him up and soothe him back to sleep before he wakes fully and becomes hysterical. It is very tricky to make this choice.

I see it as a board game: The goal is to put the baby to sleep in his crib, but to get there you first have to get him to close his eyes, then get him into a light sleep, then pick him up and carry him to bed without waking him, then put him down gently and hope that he remains asleep. If he wakes up at any point, you proceed directly to "Go" and start all over again.

I elect to pat him gently on the back. I lose. He begins to cry, and then to scream. I sigh and take him back to "Go."

Within another hour his eyes are once more closed, his head is against my chest, my cheek and nose are against his soft and fragrant hair. I am considering picking him up again and tiptoeing to the bassinet, when something eerie happens:

Without warning, Zack snaps his eyes open, raises his head, looks straight at me and grins. I am flabbergasted. It is such a knowing and happy smile I want to cry. It is also very surreal and spooky.

The smile broadens. His mouth laughs a silent laugh, as if the two of us are sharing some fantastic secret joke. And then, as suddenly as it arrived, the smile is gone, I have lost it, he has clearly forgotten our brief and heart-stopping connection, and he is once more just a newborn baby bawling his head off.

*

Babies just naturally and instinctively smile at faces—pictured, sculpted, or real . . . As early as 1946, Dr. Rene Spitz indicated that two- to six-month olds are satisfied with any face. They will smile freely to a scowling face or to an ugly mask with its tongue poking back and forth through the mouth slit.
—*The First Twelve Months of Life*, ed. by Frank Caplan, p. 55.

*

April 22. The first really warm day of the year. The trees all over town, which were bare yesterday, have suddenly erupted into little yellow green leaves. There are yellow-green weeping willows, white dogwoods, pink cherry trees, and huge pink tulip trees, none of which were in bloom yesterday. When we were in Sag Harbor last Friday the trees were already blooming there and I wondered why they weren't in East Hampton. Well, now they are. It is as if somebody just came over from Sag Harbor and switched them on.

Despite the euphoria over spring, this is the seventh day of Zack's diarrhea, and we are concerned that he might be getting dehydrated. We take him into Dr. Schonfeld to get weighed and examined.

The receptionist tells us that several children in the waiting room are quite sick, and we are not anxious to expose Zack to their germs, so I send Suzanne to wait with the baby in the car.

Three quarters of an hour later, I hear a baby crying somewhere in one of the doctors' offices. This baby is crying in the same angry, frantic, hysterical way that Zack does, and listening to it makes me think that Zack must not be worse than others his age. The more I hear this baby scream, the happier I become. And then the outside door opens, Suzanne enters with a howling Zack, and I realize that the reason the crying baby sounded so much like my son is that he was.

Dr. Schonfeld is still wearing a leotard top, jeans, clogs, and a waist length braid, and she still looks fifteen years old.

She examines Zack. He weighs 9 pounds 7 ounces, which means he has gained exactly what he should have gained since his last weighing, which means he has lost no weight from his diarrhea and Suzanne is once more validated as a good breast-feeder. His temperature, which she has taken under his arm, is normal. She examines his most recent poopy diapers, which she has asked us to bring her, and pronounced his stools within the realm of normalcy. According to Dr. Schonfeld, he does not have either diarrhea or a virus—he has been redefined into health.

What about his colic? That, says Dr. Schonfeld, he will have until he is twelve weeks old. *Twelve* weeks! I have been told colic only lasts *eight* weeks. No, says Dr. Schonfeld, twelve weeks is the age at which most babies who have colic generally grow out of it.

I take out my calendar. Zack will be twelve weeks old on May 31. How are we going to be able to survive until May 31?

*

April 23. Suzanne and I have an important business meeting in New York today. We are being auditioned for a very big writing job. The person who is interviewing us would probably not be too impressed to be doing so while Zack sucked on Suzanne.

Dr. Schonfeld has told us it will be OK to leave Zack with Karen in East Hampton. She will give him formula, and Suzanne will express and store milk at certain critical points during the day.

Five minutes before the meeting is supposed to start, Suzanne feels she is about to burst. She goes into the bathroom with her breast pump and expresses about three ounces of milk.

*

April 24, morning, Karen informs us that Zack was not at all colicky while we were gone yesterday. Could his colic be an adverse reaction to his parents?

Henry Winkler calls from California. We had worked together on a film a few years ago, and he and his wife Stacey and Suzanne and I became friends.

Henry has three kids and is very emotional about them. He is calling to say how moved he was when I phoned about Zack's birth and told him how I felt about becoming a father. I tell him about the moment of Zack's secret smile.

"This is just the beginning," he says. "You're not going to *believe* how wonderful it gets. You're not going to *believe* what's in store for you."

I have never heard anybody talk about fatherhood as positively as Henry. I think he must be a lot more patient than I am.

Zack does not seem colicky today. About the only time he has cried so far, in fact, occurred when I changed his diaper and he began to pee and it shot into his mouth.

Suzanne is playing with him after his early evening feeding. She is sitting on the rocker and Zack is lying on her knees, facing her. He puts his arms over his head. Suzanne puts her arms over her head. Zack breaks into the most amazing smile. He drops his arms and then raises them over his head again. Suzanne mimics him and he seems to find this hilarious. They raise their arms over their heads and lower them repeatedly. Zack laughs out loud.

I am transfixed by this play session. I do not think Suzanne could get the same response from him wearing an ugly mask with its tongue poking back and forth through the mouth slit. It is the first time I have seen Zack having fun. It is the first time I have seen direct and continuing interaction between one of us and Zack. And it is the first time he has seemed, for more than two seconds, to be a real little person rather than a loaf of bread. Henry, you are right.

*

April 25. For the third day in succession Zack has exhibited no signs of colic. Dare we hope that it is gone? Or is he just teasing us?

*

April 26. A fourth day with no colic—it is definitely gone! It was entitled to last twelve weeks and it only lasted six! Let the word go forth that the plague known as the colic is no more, and we are saved!

*

April 27. Our cousins Eric and Carol arrive for the weekend

with their baby, Jordan. The two tots look remarkably alike, although Jordan, who is only twelve days younger than Zack, is noticeably smaller and less active. And Jordan hardly cries at all.

We are anxious to introduce the babies and see how they react to each other. They react not at all. They look right past each other at the adults who hold them. But when Zack cries Jordan hears it and is fascinated. And when Jordan cries Zack is similarly intrigued. They can't seem to figure out where that crying is coming from—they look like they think it's themselves.

We sit Eric and Carol down in the bedroom and make them look at all the pictures we took of the pregnancy, the delivery and the baby, and we make them watch our growing videotape of Zack. The tape is currently forty minutes long, but if they are bored they are too polite to say so. I suspect they are not bored. I suspect they are as grateful as we are to be able to find someone who is willing to talk ad nauseam about babies.

We try to get Zack and Jordan to look at each other on camera, but it's hopeless. Even touching faces, they are completely invisible to the other. I suppose that makes sense—there is no survival need at this age for a baby to know what another baby is. If you are a baby, another baby cannot feed you.

*

April 29. Suzanne and I watch a powerful movie on TV called "Adam." It is a true story about a little boy named Adam who disappears in a shopping mall and is never seen again. The police are called in and Adam's parents go berserk. Then Adam's decapitated body is found—he has been kidnapped, sodomized, and beheaded by a child molester.

I find the movie so disturbing I can barely manage to watch it. I do not think that murderers of children should be executed by the state. I think they should be tortured to death by their victims' parents.

*

April 30. Zack is sleeping longer now between his feedings, and crying less. He cries mostly when he first wakes up and then when he is tired and ready to go back to sleep.

Karen, who in her last job had three children to take care of, says she feels guilty that she isn't doing more. Suzanne and I have been feeling guilty that Karen is doing too much.

*

May 1. Suzanne is feeling frisky. After breast-feeding Zack she still has quite a bit of milk left. She comes up to where I am working and squirts me in the face with it.

*

May 4, evening. Suzanne is nursing Zack. "I love breast-feeding," she says. We have come a long way.

*

May 5. We have not been too good about putting Zack in his infant seat when we take him in the car. He is still so small that he slumps to one side in it, and it is so uncomfortable it makes him cry. For short trips, the one of us who is not driving sometimes holds him.

Today, I am driving and Suzanne is holding him. We are at a stoplight in the main intersection of East Hampton, and we notice that a motorcycle cop has pulled up alongside our car and is waiting for the light to change. Suzanne slowly draws her jacket up to shield Zack from the officer's view. Infant Seat Outlaws—the Scourge of East Hampton.

*

May 6, morning. In order to be on schedule, Zack should get his dreaded DPT shot within the next day or two, but we have both been putting off phoning the pediatrician to make the appointment. I finally realize I can't procrastinate any longer, and make the call today, only to be told that they won't have an opening for at least two weeks. Now the worry is that damage will result not from the shot itself, but from his having to wait two weeks to get it.

Suzanne opens another baby gift—a corduroy outfit which looks immense. I observe that it ought to fit him by the time he's six years old. Suzanne looks at me peculiarly, then bursts into tears.

"Why are you crying?" I ask, alarmed.

"It's a twelve-month size," she explains.

The thought that Zack will be big enough to fit this huge outfit by the time he is twelve months old saddens me too, but not enough to cry.

✳

May 6, afternoon. It is time to clip the cats' claws, and Zack's. He is getting so strong it's hard to hold his hand still while cutting his fingernails. His tiny grip is so powerful it's almost painful. One of the books I read claims this is a holdover from when we were monkeys, and babies had to grip their mothers' backs so they didn't fall off. Zack almost always has hold of Suzanne's or Karen's long hair, and afterwards has strands of hair wound so tightly around his fingers they are nearly impossible to remove.

✳

May 8. Zack is two months old today.

Suzanne notices that the branches of a tree are preventing her rose garden from getting the sun. She saws off a limb, and when it falls to the ground, out tumbles a robin's nest with four tiny blue eggs. Suzanne picks up the nest and tears are in her eyes. The eggs are smashed.

"I'm a mother and I killed another mother's babies," she says, weeping.

I gently take the nest out of her hands.

"What is that mother robin going to do when she finds her nest and her eggs gone?"

I try to reassure her that mother robins don't feel the loss of their babies very keenly, but I am not certain that I believe it myself.

Later in the day Suzanne sees a robin on the lawn.

"Look at her," she says. "She's looking for her babies. God, I feel so awful."

*

May 9. Suzanne says that Zack has a great sense of humor. I ask her why she thinks so. She smiles.

"Because I tell him funny things and he laughs."

*

May 10. Karen consistently leaves the TV and the lights on in her room when she goes out of the house. I lecture her about saving energy. Then I feel uncomfortably parental. I go back and tell her she is doing such a great job with Zack that she can leave the TV and the lights on if she likes.

*

May 12. Mother's Day. I buy Suzanne a rose, and Zack has me pick her a bunch of dandelions.

*

May 13. While lying in bed on his stomach, Zack picks his head up for the first time and looks around. It is a major accomplishment. It makes him look like a turtle.

Linda Lavin phones from Los Angeles. She is throwing a surprise party for Kip's fortieth birthday on May 25th, and wants us to come. Well, Suzanne is breast-feeding, so if we came we'd have to bring Zack. And if we brought Zack, we'd want to bring Karen. Linda says she has room for all of us. We say we'll let her know.

Can you take a two-month-old baby cross-country on an airplane? The pediatrician assures us that we can. And we and Linda and Kip have shared most of the big events in each other's lives: we went to Los Angeles for their wedding, they were in New York for our baby shower, and they were the first civilians to see Zack the night he was born. We decide to go to Los Angeles.

In order to get to Los Angeles in time for the party we will have to take an 8:30 A.M. flight from JFK on May 25, which means we will have to leave East Hampton no later than 6:00 A.M. for the drive to JFK, which means we will have to get up no later than 4:30 A.M. It will hardly pay to go to bed the night before.

*

May 14. Zack is beginning to lose clumps of hair from the back and sides of his head. It is normal for this age, but it looks funny. Perhaps we could enroll him in Hair Club for Men.

*

May 15. Zack's sleeping habits have improved. He is not Sleeping Through the Night—that all but unattainable dream of most parents of tiny tots—but for the past few days he has been having a long sleep, from 7:00 P.M. to 2:00 A.M. If we wanted to end our day at 7:00 P.M. and begin it at 2:00 A.M., we could be getting seven hours of sleep every night.

We have planned a romantic evening alone. Monitoring Zack by means of a recently acquired Fisher-Price walkie-talkie, we have a quiet, candlelit dinner with wine, then take a Jacuzzi together by candlelight, and proceed to bed. But hearing Zack's every whimper, snort, and cry on the monitor is not remotely conducive to romance, and the romantic evening terminates unromantically.

*

May 18. For the past two days, Suzanne, Zack, Karen, and I have been in New York. It has proven necessary to move the mountain of junk that is piled up to the living room ceiling away from the wall it is leaning against so that the painters can paint.

Suzanne and I have recruited our friends Lee Frank and Mark McIntyre to help us move the mess away from the living room wall, and to haul our desks and filing cabinets up two flights of steps from what used to be our office and is now the baby's room to what used to be the greenhouse and is now our office.

Suzanne, Zack, Karen, and I are staying in the apartment of our long-suffering downstairs neighbor, Larry Albert, and Karen has her first opportunity to really see the New York she is so apprehensive about.

Karen takes Zack for a walk in his stroller and somehow loses her way and ends up in the middle of Times Square. Within a relatively short period of time, a crazy man drops his pants in front of her and defecates, and another man gets stabbed in the chest and runs about, shrieking and bleeding.

I have lived in New York twenty-three years and have been spared these experiences, but Karen, who is terrified of the city, encounters them both in the first hour. We have been terribly anxious for Karen to form a positive impression of New York, and it is going to take a bit of doing to compensate for the defecating and the stabbing.

After an exhausting day of lifting and carrying and breathing in plaster dust, we repair to Larry's apartment to wash up and get ready for dinner. I finish showering and dressing, and as I enter Larry's living room I realize with a hopeless, sinking feeling that Mark is holding forth to Karen on a topic he apparently knows quite well: raw sewage in New York rivers.

Mark is a reporter for *Newsday*, and his beat is, I think,

Pollution. What he seems to be in the middle of telling this apprehensive New Zealander whose experience of New York is thus far confined to public pooping and stabbing is that the sewage of a million-and-a-half New Yorkers is never treated and that their toilets flush directly into the Hudson and East Rivers. If you take a boat down the Hudson or the East River, Mark is telling her, you can see the turds bobbing in the water and clinging to the boat's hull.

This is the point at which I give up any prayer we ever had of convincing Karen to like New York. As it happens, we never had one.

*

May 20. We are back in East Hampton. Today is the day of the dreaded DPT shot. Last night Zack Slept Through the Night. Will getting a shot today be negative reinforcement for his sleeping through the night?

Dr. Schonfeld says that Zack's weight is perfect this month, right on the curve of the chart, but his length is slightly below the curve. Does this mean he's going to be short? A short bald son?

Zack gets the shot in his thigh and screams impressively. Dr. Schonfeld says if there is going to be a reaction it will occur within two to six hours. His leg could swell, and he could get a fever, but she requests that we not call her up and tell her how high the fever is.

He stops crying by the time we get him home, and we begin to wait. I am not worried about swelling or fever; I am worried about the other terrific reactions mentioned as unlikely possibilities in the literature we got at the doctor's office, like seizures.

Within two hours Zack's leg has swelled up and the area around the injection has gotten red. He is fussy and feels hot. We take his temperature. Despite the liquid Tylenol we have given him, he has a fever of 102.2, and we are nervous.

By nightfall, he is acting a little better, and the temperature is slightly lower. There is no sign of seizure or anything else. We begin to relax.

Eric and Carol call to report that they took Jordan to the Russian Tea Room, where he was perfectly behaved. Not only that, Jordan has pulled ahead of Zack in both length and weight, and has now graduated to the larger size of disposable diaper.

When we get off the phone, we realize we are jealous of Jordan's accomplishments. We discuss calling Eric and Carol back and, in mid-conversation, yelling at Zack to stop walking round the room in his noisy shoes.

*

May 21. Zack's fever and swelling and the rest of the reactions to the DPT shot have disappeared, but he is generally fussy and steadfastly refuses to take Suzanne's breast. Suzanne feels rejected and depressed and teary and says she is a failure as a mother. I think she is getting the colic.

*

May 25. It is quite dark when we arise at 4:30 A.M. to get dressed and begin loading the Jeep with baggage and baby gear for our trip to Los Angeles. In addition to our five large suitcases we are taking the collapsible Maclaren stroller, the collapsible Snugli carry-bed, and a huge box of 90 Luvs diapers with a carrying handle. I used to pity people who travelled like this.

By 6:00 A.M. we are loaded into the car and on our way to JFK, and Zack begins to cry. He continues to cry, off and on, until we arrive at the airport at 8:00 A.M.

I drop off Suzanne and Zack and Karen with all our luggage and then park the Jeep in a lot, right next to the ticket booth to minimize the chances of it being stolen, and before I lock up I put black tape over the cassette deck to discourage cassette deck thieves. There is an excellent chance that, upon our return to JFK three days hence, we will find either the cassette deck or the Jeep has been taken as a souvenir. (Chances are, it isn't an either/or situation. Chances are, if they take the Jeep they are going to take the cassette deck too.)

Zack is too fascinated with all the activity in the airport to cry. At the check-in desk I ask whether we need to check the stroller or whether we can take it on board. The agent says we can take it on board. We proceed to our gate and, for the first time in my life, I get to stand up when they make the announcement that passengers with small children who require special assistance may board early.

As soon as we are on the plane, a male stewardess informs us that strollers may not be taken on board, and takes it away from us. I explain that we'd been assured we could take the stroller with us, but the male stewardess is not even listening.

We occupy three seats abreast in the first row of the Tourist Class cabin. The couple on Karen's left is on its honeymoon and appears to be at least theoretically pro-baby, but the guy on my right is definitely pissed to be travelling next to an infant. In fact, he is so furious he refuses to look at any of us, and Zack hasn't even started crying yet.

It's funny—I used to be the guy on my right. Well, I put up with other people's babies on planes for several decades, and now other people can put up with mine, and if the guy on my right is pissed, let him become a father too.

Shortly after takeoff Zack begins to scream. While I am adjusting his carry-bed in the area of Karen's seat, a cup of tomato juice which had been resting on the arm of Suzanne's seat falls off and spills all over Karen's new white slacks and all over the outfit of the honeymooning bride to Karen's left.

Karen and the honeymoon bride are thoroughly spattered with tomato juice. I rush to get napkins and bottles of club soda from the stewardess to try and take out the stains.

Karen is fuming. The honeymooning bride is terribly decent about the whole thing, but Suzanne notices that she is crying. It is not clear who is to blame for the tomato juice, but it is most likely me and I feel terrible. I tell Karen that if the stains in her slacks don't come out I will buy her new ones.

Zack continues to scream, Karen continues to fume, the bride continues to cry. The guy on my right is wound up so tight he is ready to pop. Suzanne and I are wearing extremely strained smiles. I ask Suzanne, who is normally frightened of flying, if she is afraid.

"To tell the truth," she replies, "I wouldn't mind all that much if we crashed."

By and by, the vibration of the plane's engines soothes Zack. He settles down, stops crying, falls asleep, and is a model baby for the duration of the flight. When we land at LAX, the stewardess says what a good baby he was.

When the baggage comes off the carousel, we get back all five suitcases and the box of 90 Luvs diapers, but Suzanne realizes we don't have the stroller. I race all the way back to the plane before it takes off again, and breathlessly explain to the agent at the gate that our stroller is on board. He is quite pleasant about it, being a father himself, and takes me aboard the plane.

But the stroller is not on board, and the male stewardess who took it away from me says he checked it. I tell him it was not on the baggage carousel, and he says it may have been put on a later plane. If I will just go down to the lost baggage office, they will be able to tell me what happened to it.

But the agent at the lost baggage office can offer no advice other than that the stroller will probably be arriving in three hours or so, and we can come back to the airport at our convenience and pick it up.

We explain that the trip from where we are staying at Linda's to the airport and back will take two hours, and the concept of convenience does not apply. The agent says we could have the stroller delivered to us where we are staying, but that will cost us $35.

Keeping my voice amazingly calm, I tell the agent that one of her fellow employees in New York had assured us we could take the stroller on board, or else we'd have checked it with the rest of our baggage and we would have it now, and we wouldn't need to spend either two hours or $35 to get it back.

The agent is only half listening to me, because she is having a much worse time with a couple who lost all their baggage and who are en route to Hawaii with no hope at all of ever getting it back. The baggageless couple become abusive in their desperation, and when they leave I am so calm by comparison that the agent agrees to send us our stroller without charge. I thank her profusely and tell her she's a better person than she'd heard.

We rent a car with an infant carseat and drive to Linda's and Kip's and the party is a huge success. All of us were to dress as we might have appeared forty years ago, when Kip was born. The majority of the guests are show people, and there are some remarkably inventive outfits. There is also a dance band that plays 1940s music, a singer who sounds exactly like Frank Sinatra, a trio who sound exactly like the Andrew Sisters, and Kip claims to be surprised.

The dancing and music go on quite late, and when we finally get to bed I calculate we have been up for twenty-four hours in succession.

*

May 27. It is a beautiful sunny California day and it is decided that Linda and Kip and Kip's two brothers and Kip's two sisters-in-law and Kip's eighteen-month-old nephew and Kip's mother and Kip's Uncle Wally and Suzanne and Zack and I will all go to Venice beach.

But by the time we get to the shore and set up the now broken carry-bed and get settled it's freezing and the wind is driving sand into all our faces and Zack is screaming. After the time it has taken to get there and get settled, we are loathe to leave so soon, so we stay awhile and pretend we are having a much better time at the beach than we are.

*

May 28, night. Suzanne, Karen, Zack, and I have flown back to New York without incident—Zack even slept through the movie—but as we approach JFK airport the pilot informs us that the weather in New York is rainy and quite windy. I have something of a bias against a phenomenon known as wind shear, which comes up a lot during rainy, windy weather and which has accounted for a large percentage of recent airplane tragedies, and so I am not gladdened by this news.

I am even more unhappy when the pilot informs us over the public address system that, uh, there seems to be a minor problem, folks, so minor, really, that it's hardly even worth mentioning, but the flaps have for some reason ceased to function. "But there is absolutely no problem whatsoever, folks," he repeats, and nobody on the aircraft, even Zack, is remotely convinced of his sincerity.

Suzanne and I exchange worried glances, hold Zack very tightly, and pray. Has the trip to Los Angeles been a tragic mistake after all? Have we recklessly gambled our baby's life on a pair of faulty flaps? If the pilot really thinks that landing on a rainy, windy night with no flaps is "absolutely no problem whatsoever," then why has he even brought it up?

The plane slowly slowly descends, makes a safe, if somewhat bouncy landing, and as the pilot throws his engines into reverse to slow the aircraft, I notice that an entire convoy of firetrucks is lined up along the runway with dome lights flashing, waiting to extinguish us when we ignite, not having heard that landing on a rainy, windy night with no flaps is absolutely no problem whatsoever.

Not only have we landed safely, baby intact, but neither the Jeep nor the cassette deck have found new owners.

∗

May 30, night. Suzanne's mother and father and brother Jim have arrived from Dallas, Texas, to see Zack. Driving them back to East Hampton from Long Island's MacArthur Airport, I am seized by a peculiar notion: Her family has not seen Suzanne since before she was pregnant—how do they know we really have a baby? How do they know the whole thing hasn't been a huge hoax, the phoned reports of pregnancy and labor and delivery and homecoming and breast-feeding only elaborate contrivances, the photos we sent them posed by a borrowed baby? Could they possibly be watching me now, waiting to see how long I can maintain the charade, even up to the moment where I enter our house and, finally required to produce the child, shamefacedly admit the whole thing was an elaborate sham?

It is not, I hasten to point out, that I *believe* such galloping paranoia, it's merely that the notion has suggested itself to my fertile novelist's imagination. OK, it's not only my fertile novelist's imagination; I really am that paranoid.

We arrive at the house, Suzanne greets her family, and when they ask to see the baby, she replies that he is sleeping and they will have to wait until morning to see him. Couldn't they just tiptoe into his room and take a quick peek at him asleep? No, says Suzanne, he's a very light sleeper and it would wake him up, and then we'd never be able to get him to sleep again. Is it my imagination, or do I see them exchange covert glances?

∗

May 31, morning. We bring Zack in to meet his Grandma Irma and his Grandpapa Don and his Uncle Jim. They are ecstatic. I turn to Jim, who is 21 and has a wry sense of humor and a lively imagination of his own.

"I had this fantasy," I tell him, "that you were beginning to doubt that Zack existed."

"That :hought did cross my mind," says Jim dryly.

*

May 31, afternoon. Suzanne is holding Zack while her father watches. Zack is crying. When Suzanne herself was a baby she had colic and cried all the time.

"You're being repaid, Suzanne," says her father.

*

May 31, evening. Suzanne is breast-feeding Zack while her mother watches. Suzanne, as I have mentioned, is extremely nervous she won't have enough milk for Zack—as nervous as her mother was that she didn't have enough milk for Suzanne. After Zack nurses for awhile he seems to have some difficulty in getting milk from Suzanne's breast and begins to cry.

"Oh, there's nothing left?" says Suzanne's mother to Zack. "You're sucking death?"

I am startled, but it turns out that "sucking death" was a common expression in Suzanne's mother's family. The term referred to babies nursing at an empty breast.

*

June 1. Suzanne's father holds Zack and studies him fondly.

"I have seen that face before," he says. "I have seen that face before, and I never knew Dan as a baby."

*

June 2. Suzanne and I have taken Zack to the drugstore to pick up some more disposable diapers. Standing a few paces off is a young mother and a father with a screaming baby girl in a Snugli. The father looks at Zack and then at his daughter.

"Why can't you be quiet like *that* baby?" he says to his daughter.

Suzanne and I exchange a look and say nothing. It is the first time we have been anywhere at all that the baby who was screaming wasn't Zack.

*

June 3, morning. I tell Suzanne I read in one of our books that this is the age (about three months) that Zack is just beginning to figure out that he is a separate person—up till now he thought that he was part of her.

"That's funny," she says, smiling, "I thought I was a part of him too."

*

June 3, afternoon. We take Suzanne's mother and father and brother and Zack into New York to attend a reunion of our Lamaze class. I'm not sure what the O'Malleys are going to get out of it, but they are too good-natured to act anything but fascinated at the prospect of seeing a bunch of people they don't know and their new babies.

The Lamaze reunion is being held in a building approximately sixteen blocks from our apartment. We wheel Zack in his stroller through the normally heavy crowds and traffic and noise of midtown Manhattan, and it frightens me—there are so many awful things that can happen to anyone, especially a tiny baby, in such a place. Cabs and cars and even bicycles run stoplights and plow into pedestrians, cranes fall routinely out of midtown Manhattan construction sites and crush passersby, and deranged people in this city often assault strangers for no reason at all.

Even if no such calamities befall him, how does Zack react to all this noise and congestion at the age of three months? I am an adult and have lived in New York twenty-three years, and because I've been out of the city for several months now I find the sounds and smells of the city overpowering.

Although I feel slightly overwhelmed, Zack looks surprisingly calm, alert, and fascinated by the horns, the sirens, the entire sensory assault.

We enter the ground floor of the small East Side brownstone where the reunion is being held to find two tiny rooms and a narrow hallway choked with parents and babies—not one but three Lamaze reunions are going on simultaneously.

We have all been asked to bring wine or cheese or crackers, and we have all obediently done so. As babies squall and blubber on all sides of us, Suzanne and I sip wine out of plastic cups and try to become reacquainted with our former classmates.

It is the first time I have seen infants younger than Zack and I am amazed—I wouldn't have believed there were babies smaller than ours. There are three dozen infants here. I study the selection and am gratified to find that Zack is by far the cutest. There is only one other baby who is even close. I wonder if this obvious fact is apparent to the other parents, and, if so, how they feel about it.

A heavy-set middle-aged dad is proudly lugging around a gargantuan heavy-set baby whom he introduces as Zack. I ask the heavy-set dad how much *his* Zack weighs, and am told sixteen pounds. I can't imagine how a baby from our class could already be this big. I ask the heavy-set dad when this particular Zack was born. The heavy-set dad is momentarily thrown by my question. After some silent calculations and a brief conference with his wife, he tells me his Zack was born on June 27. As today is June 3, the child would either have to be a year old or else still be a fetus, and neither of these is likely.

A slightly distracted-looking young woman is holding a baby girl about the age of our Zack. I ask the young woman her daughter's name. She looks at me blankly a moment, blushes, and turns to her husband for help.

"Andrea," says the husband to his wife. "The baby's name is Andrea."

"I keep wanting to say 'Rebecca,' " says the woman, frowning.

"Rebecca is your niece," says the husband.

I suspect from these two encounters that there are many new moms and dads who are considerably more befuddled than we are.

Our Lamaze teacher goes from one reunion to the other, trying to socialize as expediently as possible. She squeezes into the narrow hallway where our class has been crammed and encourages us to share our experiences of delivery, but she limits our sharing to thirty seconds per couple. Thirty seconds is just about long enough to give your name, rank, and serial number. This is somehow not the warm, caring coda to the Lamaze experience that I had been led to expect.

*

June 4, morning. We take videotape footage of Zack with Grandpa Don, Grandma Irma, and Uncle Jim. On camera Grandpa Don tells Zack he plans to take him to the family farm and let him ride his tractor, which causes Zack to burst into immediate tears. On camera Grandma Irma is asked whom she thinks Zack resembles most, Dan or Suzanne. Grandma Irma studies Zack a moment and then replies in all candor, "I think he looks like *me*."

*

June 4, afternoon. An interesting baby present arrives for Zack today from our friend Jan Cobler in Los Angeles—a computer-generated horoscope called a birthprint, written by someone in Minneapolis named Lynn Burmyn ("THIS IS A LYNN BURMYN BIRTHPRINT™, written and designed by Lynn Burmyn.")

Suzanne reads the birthprint aloud to me. It describes Zack as if he were an already formed personality rather than a not-quite-three-month-old baby, and it sounds eerily accurate. For example:

Zack is a solemn, sweet child who seems to have been born with a mission he can't quite identify. . . .

Young Zack is very sensitive and may sometimes feel overwhelmed by the world around him. . . . As he is extremely aware of other people's expectations, he may try to live up to what he assumes others want, to be what they want him to be. . . .

Though occasionally he will rebel, most of the time Zack succeeds in meeting the expectations of others but ends up feeling—sometimes correctly—as if he's fooled everyone into believing he's someone he's not. From there, he may go on to believe others wouldn't accept his REAL self if they knew him, or he may feel secretly smarter than everyone else; if they've accepted his grand deception, he may despair of ever finding someone smart enough to see through the facade and take care of him properly. Even as he yearns for recognition and fears being invisible or hopelessly transparent, Zack may take great pains to hide his true self. Though he may be a pleasant and adaptable child as a result, both Zack and others may acknowledge that no one truly knows him well. Adults who encourage and applaud his differences and healthy idiosyncrasies will add immeasurably to Zack's self-esteem and sense of personhood.

It goes on like that for fifteen single-spaced typed pages, and sounds more like an observant child psychologist from the future who knew Zack several years from now and dropped by to tell us about him than a person in Minneapolis who's never met him.

*

June 5. After a lovely visit, the O'Malleys flew back to Texas yesterday. Today I have invited Suzanne to a romantic dinner. Since she is breast-feeding, our plans depend upon Zack's waking up between 6:00 and 8:00 P.M. so Suzanne can nurse him and we can then leave him with Karen and go out to dinner.

But Zack has not been informed of our plans, and refuses to wake up. We reluctantly make dinner and eat it at the kitchen counter, in the course of which Zack finally does wake up for Suzanne to feed him.

"I never would have accepted this date if I had known you had a kid," says Suzanne.

"You didn't know I had a kid?"

"I did, but I thought you only had him on the weekends."

"Well, listen, you're an awfully good sport to be breast-feeding him."

*

June 11. Karen is strangely sullen today. Suzanne and I ask independently whether anything is wrong, and Karen shakes her head negatively both times, but it is clear that she is furious about something.

*

June 12. Zack is trying to learn how to turn himself over. Yesterday and today, while lying on his stomach, he puts his behind into the air and falls down, nearly turning over in the process. It has not occurred to him that turning over can be accomplished by any other means.

*

June 14. Our cousins Eric and Carol bring Jordan back for another weekend. Jordan has undergone an amazing transformation. The last time we saw Jordan he was smaller than Zack. Now he is tremendous—fourteen-and-a-half pounds. His feet and hands and legs are considerably larger than Zack's. Suzanne and I, having heard by phone how much Jordan has grown, briefly considered going out and borrowing a year-old baby from friends and pretending it was Zack. I now regret we didn't do it.

Carol is surprised that Zack is so small. Accustomed to Jordan's weight, she picks Zack up and inadvertently hoists him halfway to the ceiling.

*

June 15. We take Zack, Jordan, Carol, and Eric to the beach, where there appears to be a baby on every blanket—there is little doubt that we are in the midst of another Baby Boom. No sooner do we get settled on our own blanket than we run into Alan and Beverly Cowan, old friends from New York. Alan and Beverly are recent parents themselves—their baby is two weeks older than Zack—and after an hour of baby anecdote swapping, we get down to some rather frank talk.

Alan and Beverly reveal that they didn't make love for two months preceding the birth of their daughter, that they have done it only three times in the three months since the birth, and that each time it has been painful as hell. I say our own experience has not been dissimilar, and Carol and Eric concur as well. Suzanne laments that when they sew up your episiotomy they make you considerably tighter than you were before. A young mother we visited on our recent trip to California confessed to us that for the first eighteen months following childbirth sex was excruciating, and she used to run when she saw her husband approaching her with a gleam in his eye.

Why doesn't anybody level with you about this? Why do the obstetricians and the guidebooks imply that you'll be having sex right up to the time you're fully dilated, and that the longest it ever takes any normal couple to get back to regular sex is six weeks? If there could be a bit more candor in this area, new parents might feel they were within the mainstream of human experience rather than candidates for the Masters and Johnson clinic.

As we chat about such matters, a man and a woman who are clearly at least nine months pregnant stop by our blanket and begin making inquiries about the babies on display. We learn that their names are Arlene and Peter and they are in fact expecting their baby in about half an hour.

I jokingly ask them to run through Stage III breathing for me, and they look uncomfortable. Frankly, says Arlene, she's never gotten around to learning the breathing and is sort of relying on Peter to remember it. Peter confesses he's never really gotten the hang of the breathing either, and I proceed to give them a crash course in all three stages of Lamaze breathing.

Arlene asks twice about the pain of childbirth. None of the mothers present is willing to reassure her in any meaningful way—when Carol was in delivery the hospital sent someone in to ask her to stop screaming because she was scaring the other women. Peter asks three times whether husbands tend to take much abuse from wives during delivery. Alan and I are able to reassure Peter on this point, but Eric merely smiles and turns to Carol, who tells Peter it depends on the wife.

We try once more to get Jordan and Zack to interact. Jordan tentatively touches Zack's hand, then takes Zack's pacifier and sticks his finger in Zack's eye.

*

June 15. Two outfits sent to Zack as presents by Suzanne's cousins are sweet, old-fashioned, and ruffled. Suzanne says she likes Zack to wear them because they make him look innocent. I find it an interesting notion, dressing a twelve-week-old infant to look innocent. How worldly could Zack look, even were he to wear black leather with zippers and links of chain? I mean what level of sophistication can you achieve when you can't sit upright and your memory is only seven seconds long?

*

June 16. Father's Day. Since Karen is off today, I get up to feed Zack a relief bottle at 4:00 and 6:00 A.M., and to change an incredible poop born of Malt-Supex baby laxative and paving tar.

To celebrate Father's Day we take Zack to the Candy Kitchen for lunch and then to a kids' store called Penny Whistle and buy him a baseball cap which looks like a duck's head, with a smoked plastic sunshade made to look like a duck's bill. Zack, in turn, buys me the traditional Father's Day gift of monogrammed handkerchieves.

*

June 17. Zack's three-month checkup at the pediatrician. He is now up to 24 inches, and 11 pounds 10 ounces. Zack steadfastedly resists all of Dr. Schonfeld's attempts to examine him.

"Babies this age aren't supposed to have control of their arms or legs," says Dr. Schonfeld, "but they always manage to push me away while I'm examining them."

*

June 18. Suzanne has to go into New York today for her regular Tuesday therapy appointment. Because Suzanne experienced spotting when going too long between feedings, Dr. Schonfeld has advised her not to be away from Zack for the whole day if she expects to continue breast-feeding. Suzanne elects to drive in with Zack.

It is not an easy trip. On two occasions at rest areas on the Long Island Expressway, truck drivers incorrectly identify Suzanne as a loose woman looking for a date and attempt to pick her up. Zack gets cranky and does a fair amount of crying. Suzanne tries to soothe him with various cassettes of popular music. Madonna doesn't do a thing for him, but a group called Wham! stops the crying every time she plays it.

Prior to this strange affinity my son displays for Wham! I had not been a huge fan of the group. I was particularly not a fan of Wham!'s big hit, "Wake Me Up Before You Go-Go." It is now one of my favorite selections.

While Suzanne is in New York with Zack, my mother arrives at MacArthur Airport for a week-long visit that will include my birthday on June 20.

Upon our arrival in East Hampton she is dismayed to learn that Zack is still in New York and she will have to wait several hours to meet him. To soften the disappointment I play her the videotape we have been making of him. For the first hour she is absolutely enchanted with every image of him on the screen. As we conclude our second hour she inquires tactfully if there is a good deal more. Fortunately there is not—even grandmas should not be subjected to more than two hours of videotape of their grandchildren. And within five minutes of the tape's end, Zack himself arrives.

Mom is obviously deeply moved at meeting Zack. And just as when I telephoned her to announce his birth, I know that part of the reason for her tears now is the thought that Dad will never know his son's son.

*

June 19. Zack notices himself in the mirror for the first time today. He smiles coyly at his image, his lips pursed like Bill Cosby, and turns away.

*

June 20. My forty-ninth birthday. I receive a wonderful birthday card from my mother. It says, "When I think of all the things that would have never been—if you had never been—I celebrate the day you were born." The same sentiment applies to Zack, and the idea that we came so close to never having him is quite a sobering one.

I must confess that birthdays no longer fill me with glee, and being a father of forty-nine leads me to gloomy questions about the future: What age will I be when Zack first begins to think of me as an old fart, and, worse yet, will he be right? I will probably see him graduate college, but will I live to dance at his wedding? And is there a chance I will ever be alive to see a child of his, or will I die before that happens, as did my own father?

Such questions are not useful, and seem the musings of a man far older than I look and act and feel and am. Indeed, I can scarcely afford to think about aging and dying while I am still involved in the full-time job of growing up.

A couple of weeks ago I awoke to the first really warm day of the year and, although hot weather has always been my favorite, the realization that summer was about to begin filled me with sadness for the first time. I could not immediately think why, and then, gradually, it came to me.

The happiest days of my childhood were spent with my Mom and Dad in the Indiana Dunes. The first few summers of my life we shared a cabin at the edge of Lake Michigan with friends.

The cabin was little more than a shack. It had neither plumbing nor electricity, but I thought that pumps, outhouses, and kerosene lanterns were far more interesting than running water, indoor toilets, and electric lights. I have powerful and pleasant memories of being in that cabin and on the beach and in the water with my mom and dad, and these have been endlessly reinforced by snapshots and 8 mm. films my dad took of us during those periods.

I guess that the onset of summer this year, the first summer of my fatherhood, made me realize at some primal, subconscious level that I will never again be taken care of and taught and protected and adored in the wonderful way I remember from those summers in the Indiana Dunes—that, in fact, *I* am the father now, and I must take care of and teach and protect my son as my father did for me.

I know that that is appropriate, that I am equal to the task, that I will even enjoy it, that I have been taking care of and teaching and protecting myself for years and years, but still the realization that I must now forever relinquish the role of son is what I think made me feel empty and sad. Now that I know where the feeling came from, I hope I am better able to deal with it on a conscious and mature level and to move on.

*

June 21. Two firsts for Zack today: the first time he laughs out loud, and the first time he succeeds in putting both fists into his mouth simultaneously.

*

June 23. We have been warned by the county health office about ticks. Ticks are plentiful at this time of year, and they can carry Rocky Mountain Spotted Fever, a dreadful disease. I have been fairly careful to check our cats for ticks whenever they come into the house. Every other time I check I find a tick, which I kill and flush down the toilet.

Our neighbor Ian Hornak calls to say that a man in the nearby East Hampton section of Springs has just died of Rocky Mountain Spotted Fever which he got from a tick bite. It isn't possible to catch all the ticks the cats bring in or to make sure the ticks don't find their way to Zack, but we must try.

*

June 24, morning. In a discussion with Mom today I learn something about Dad which surprises me. I had always been told that Dad was reluctant to have kids because he wasn't sure it was fair to bring a child into the world of the early 1930s.

In today's discussion Mom reveals that it wasn't only fears about the Depression and war that gave Dad pause about having kids, that Dad had many of the same fears about fatherhood I'd had myself, and that the only reason they decided to go ahead and have me was that Mom insisted. And now the sentiment in Mom's birthday card is even more meaningful to me.

*

June 24, evening. We make a videotape of Mom with Zack and encourage her to sing to him the same Yiddish and Russian lullabies she used to sing to me when I was a baby. As she begins to croon, in a voice that makes me shiver with nostalgia, Zack is absolutely fascinated and listens with great intensity to every syllable.

*

June 25. It is almost exactly a year since Zack was conceived. He is three-and-a-half months old. We leave Karen in East Hampton and drive in to New York to show Mom our mostly renovated apartment, and to show Zack his new room and crib. Suzanne and I put Zack down on his stomach for his first nap in his new crib and he immediately turns himself over on his back for the first time. We are amazed, and delighted that we both saw it happen together, and we decide that his turning over the first time he was put down in his new crib is a good omen.

We congratulate Zack on his feat, and then we put him back on his stomach. He turns over a second time. We go and get my Mom to show her Zack's new trick. We put him back on his stomach, but by now he has completely forgotten how he did it.

Mom leaves to spend time with a friend of hers, and Suzanne goes off to some appointments, and while they are gone Zack is restless, wakeful, and cranky. By the time Suzanne returns, I am pretty cranky myself. She asks me how Zack was while she was gone.

"He wet through six diapers and two stretchies and his sheet and his quilt, and he didn't sleep for more than twenty minutes," I reply.

She considers this a moment.

"I guess what you're trying to tell me," she says, "is that you're a good father and you work hard to take care of your son."

I nod, grateful for her understanding.

*

June 27. Another milestone. Zack has gotten big enough to change to the next size of disposable diaper—"Crawler, 12–26 lbs." instead of "Newborn, 6–12 lbs." He also takes the occasion to turn himself over again, from his stomach to his back. One gets the impression that the feat was accomplished by trial and error and not by memory. Since his memory is still reputed to be about seven seconds, this is not surprising.

*

June 28, morning. Our fifth wedding anniversary. Caldor's has advertised a special on baby photographs. If we bring our baby in for a special shooting today, for just $8.88 they will give us fifteen wallet-sized photos, three 5 × 7s and two 8 × 10s in a variety of poses. We have no illusions about what the quality of the photographs will be—at $8.88 it's worth the gamble.

Aware that the lighting and focus will be classic and old-fashioned, we dress him in a classic and old-fashioned sailor suit. The photo area when we get to Caldor's is set up with painted backdrops. The photographer, a garrulous fellow in his mid-30s, calls Zack "Smiley" and swiftly poses him along with Suzanne, who has also worn a classic and old-fashioned sailor suit for the occasion.

The photographer is so smooth and so assured and so good at making Zack smile I am positive he has kids of his own.

"Oh no," he says, shaking off the thought, "I'm on the road forty-eight weeks a year taking pictures of kids, and that's enough for me."

He requests a deposit from us and says we'll be sent a postcard when our pictures are ready.

Later in the day I phone my sister Naomi in Sycamore, Illinois, to tell her about the Caldor photo session and to marvel at how they are able to give you all those photos for just $8.88.

Naomi has participated in similar photo offers where she lives. The deal, she says, is that when you come in to see your photos they try to sell you additional enlargements for substantially more money. Naomi says she realized that whatever she didn't buy they'd throw out, and she couldn't bear the idea of photos of her children being tossed in the garbage, so she bought whatever they offered her. I resolve to be more cold-blooded.

*

June 29, evening. Our first big dinner party since Zack's birth. A guest named Clay Felker who is not known for extravagant statements about small children studies Zack for several moments and then solemnly proclaims our son one of the most beautiful babies he has ever seen.

A guest named Julie Baumgold warns us of the day when we get on the birthday party circuit: "You'll spend all your time in Penny Whistle buying presents."

A guest named Avery Corman (whom you'll remember as the chap who warned me never to get my son a dog) appears depressed. When I ask what is wrong he tells me he sent his two sons off to camp for the first time today. Not only that, but one of them, Matthew, will no longer allow Avery to hold his hand or to hug him.

I recall that when we were on Venice beach with Linda and Kip and their family, we noticed that Kip's sister-in-law made up an intricate pony game to play with her son, which was little more than an excuse to get some furtive hugs from a toddler who no longer wanted them.

After the party Suzanne and I give Zack his late feeding and once more marvel at this person we have created. I tell her it's hard, sometimes, to think he is our son and not some terrific science project that we made together.

*

June 30. While Suzanne is breast-feeding Zack in the kitchen this morning, she notices that he is smiling delight-edly at something up near the ceiling. We look in the direction he is smiling and, of course, see nothing.

A bit lower than where he is staring hangs a string of dried jalapeño peppers someone gave us, and we erroneously decide that this is what he finds so amusing. But it is not the peppers which tickle him so, it is something else. Something above the peppers. Some invisible friend, perhaps. What could he be seeing? People who believe in ghosts or angels would have no problem identifying what Zack is seeing. Watching him smile and giggle at this unseen entity is a little eerie.

Suzanne dubs Zack's invisible friend Mr. Peppers. I would give a lot to know what—or who—it is.

*

July 1. Suzanne is breast-feeding Zack and talking to him in the next room. This is what she is saying to him:

"Zack, I just love the fact that you have no teeth. I don't ever want you to have teeth, or crawl, or stand up, or walk, or go on dates, or get married. I want you to stay right here with me and be my baby."

*

July 3. It is Karen's day off. I get up at 4:50 and 6:50 A.M. to feed Zack. Today is the first time I have seen him hold himself in a sitting position. He cannot hold it for long, but he is definitely doing it. In the meantime he has completely forgot-ten how to turn himself over, although he continues to try.

*

July 6. Totally by accident, Zack turns himself over today. He is astonished.

When he is being nursed in the kitchen he still smiles and giggles at Mr. Peppers. We still don't know what it is he sees.

*

July 7. This evening we have been invited to the home of our friend John Huszar for dinner. It is Karen's day off, and we are nervous about taking Zack to a dinner party, but John says it is OK. The Swyngomatic is currently the device that stops Zack from crying most effectively. We drive to John's house in the Porsche with the top down, with Zack in his infant seat, and with the huge Swyngomatic upside down and sticking ludicrously into the air. Others cars pass us and their occupants snicker at us.

The Swyngomatic entrances Zack out of crying at John's dinner party for approximately ninety seconds. We put Zack in an upstairs bedroom, and for most of the evening Suzanne and I take turns staying with him and trying to get him to sleep.

*

July 9. Zack is four months old. Suzanne has read in the guidebooks that at this age Zack should have a favorite toy. He has thus far displayed little or no interest in the scores of toys we've offered him, and we have become concerned.

Suzanne takes Zack into New York for the day on the Hampton Jitney, and when she returns she is ecstatic:

"Guess what? Zack has a favorite toy—the bunny rattle your mom gave him. He reaches for it with both hands, he puts it in his mouth, and he cries when he thinks it's gone."

"What do you mean when he thinks it's gone?"

"Oh, he thinks it's gone whenever he can't see it—when it

falls on his chest under his chin, or when it falls to one side while he's still holding it."

*

The baby under nine months doesn't seem to have the slightest notion that an object has an independent existence, that it exists whether he sees it or not. This goes for human objects—his parents, members of his household—and it applies to his bottle, his toys, the furniture—in short, any object in his limited world. When the object disappears from view it ceases to exist. The baby does not imagine that it is *some* place, that it exists whether or not he sees it.
—*The Magic Years*, Selma H. Fraiberg, p. 48.

*

July 10. Giant ants descended upon us a couple of days ago and have now totally disappeared. This morning we have been engulfed by what Suzanne refers to as earwigs—little black caterpillar-like bugs with two horn-like protuberances at the tail. They have appeared as mysteriously as the giant ants, and are slightly more disgusting-looking. We do our best to get rid of them.

A photographer from *Newsday* comes over in the early afternoon to photograph Suzanne and Zack and me for an article on pregnancy in the Sunday section for which Suzanne was interviewed. When the photographer arrives he casually remarks how beautiful Zack is and how much he looks like me. Two hours after he leaves Suzanne says to me: "I can't believe that photographer walked right in here and said that Zack looked like *you*."

*

July 11, morning. The earwigs are mostly gone, but in their place we have large winged ants—considerably smaller than the giant ants, but far greater in number. They crawl around the screen doors by the thousands. They are slow-moving and easy to kill, but they are present in astonishing numbers.

I know we live in the woods and that these creatures find it hard to comprehend the division between indoors and outdoors, but this still does not explain the appearance of so many of them at a single time. Is it the convention season? Is it God visiting plagues upon us to make us let our indentured servants go? Whom would God have us let go?

Probably Karen. Karen has grown increasingly difficult as time progresses. From the first she has taken on gardening chores we have not asked her to do, but she has been doing them in a haphazard manner. Plants which we told her need to be watered three times a week she waters once a week or not at all, plants which we told her need to be watered once a week she waters almost every day, and so we discover that most of our plants have been dying of either thirst or rot.

The way Karen makes fruit juice out of concentrate is to empty the can of concentrate into a large juice container, and then fill the container up with water. It doesn't matter to her how big or small the can of concentrate is, the same amount of water goes in the container. The result is juice that is either almost pure water or juice as thick as porridge.

She is openly resentful when we try to get her to do things our way. She sulks, she gives us the silent treatment, she slams doors. She is still great with Zack, but not with us. When she first came to us she was a saint.

In one last effort to get Karen to shape up, Suzanne has typed a lengthy and quite detailed outline of her duties and left it on the kitchen counter. We don't know what effect it will have.

*

July 11, evening. Suzanne overheard in the next room playing Simon Says with Zack:

"Simon says touch your toes. Simon says claps your hands.

Simon says clap your feet. Simon says sleep through the night."

*

July 12, morning. The winged ants have been replaced by clouds of tiny gnats. They hover at the screen doors trying to get in. I spray insecticide at them and it blows back into the house, making me fear its effect on Zack.

Karen has read the detailed list of her duties and is in a black rage. Whether out of anger or ignorance, this morning she threw into the trash several stems of rubrum lilies from Suzanne's lily garden which were not nearly ready for the garbage. Both Suzanne and I are angry at the waste. When I mention to Karen that the lilies weren't ready to be thrown out yet, she snaps that it isn't a good time to talk. I disagree. I say it is the *perfect* time to talk.

Karen's accumulated anger at us spills out—she resents the typed list of duties, as it includes things she has volunteered to do, like gardening, which are not part of her job. She resents being told what to do and how to do it. She says we're too demanding, too messy, our house is too small, our friends are phony, and she hates when we give her compliments because she doesn't believe any compliments are ever sincere. She is leaving on November 1, she informs us, instead of March 15.

We suggest to her that November 1 might not be soon enough, and call the agency in Vancouver to ask for someone to replace Karen as quickly as possible.

*

July 12, evening. Tonight Suzanne and I have arranged to take a class at Southampton Hospital in baby C.P.R. (cardiopulmonary resuscitation), called Babylife. Karen is not available to babysit and so we ask a neighbor if we can bring Zack over on the way to class, and then pick him up after it. The neighbor is agreeable, and, although she has several children of her own, we are apprehensive because this is the first time we have ever left Zack with anybody but Karen.

The class takes place in a room with a long conference table. Seated around the table are a paramedic named Noel Merenstein and about fifteen parents. Merenstein tells us sobering stories of babies and toddlers who had stopped breathing and who were brought back to life by this training. Then he gives each of us a life-sized rubber doll in a blue-and-white-striped outfit with which to practice what he teaches us. In an emergency, it is not the theories but the hands-on experience with the doll which we will remember, he says.

The ABCs of baby C.P.R. arc similar to those for adults: Airway, Breathing, and Circulation. If you believe a child is in distress you say, "Baby, baby, are you all right?", you pinch him and watch for a response.

If there is no response, you check his Airway: You put him on his back, quickly examine his mouth for obstructions, then tilt his head backward, clearing the passage of air to his lungs.

Then you check for Breathing: You put your ear to his mouth and listen for breath, at the same time looking at his chest to see if it is moving. If not, you cover his nose and lips with your mouth and blow forcefully four times, taking your lips away from his face each time.   Then you check for Circulation: You feel the inside of his closest arm, just below the bicep, for a pulse, while counting to ten. If you feel no pulse, you find his sternum, midway between his nipples, and, taking three stiff fingers of your right hand, you press on the sternum rapidly five times. Then you combine the Breathing and the Circulation—one forceful breath into his mouth, five thrusts of your fingers against his sternum, one breath, five thrusts, and so on—all the while checking for signs of life and carrying him to the phone and calling for an ambulance.

At intermission, knowing how much Zack cries and how difficult it is for him to sleep, I call our neighbor to see how he is doing. She says it is always hard for a parent to hear this, but our baby has been perfect—he hasn't cried once, and he fell asleep immediately. I go back to the class.

Merenstein drills us repeatedly on his Babylife techniques. I am alternately chilled at the thought of ever having to employ these techniques on our baby, and amused at the ludicrous sight of fifteen adults blowing repeatedly into the mouths of fifteen rubber dolls wearing blue-and-white-striped outfits.

When we finish I feel we have learned something exceedingly valuable.

*

July 13. The latest plague is a barrage of ants so tiny they are almost invisible. Since the slaves have been released, I hardly see the point.

It is extremely awkward living in the same house with Karen following our fight. It is like breaking up with your mate and not being able to move out. Suzanne is so uncomfortable at the prospect of encountering Karen in the kitchen she confines herself to our bedroom and complains she feels a prisoner in her own house.

But Karen continues to be great with Zack, playing with him in a manner so joyous and free that I wish I could duplicate it. When Karen is with him she always gives him her full attention. When I am with him I am often distracted, trying to do something else at the same time. I must take Karen's example and learn to be totally with Zack when I am with him.

*

July 14, afternoon. Zack already has a full-sized crib in the city, but in East Hampton he is still sleeping in his tiny bassinet, or in his electric rocking cradle which ceased rocking electrically months ago. In any case, both of these are too small for him now, and we have been promised the loan of a full-sized crib by Bruce Jay Friedman and his wife Pat O'Donohue.

We take Zack to Bruce and Pat's to pick up the crib. Their daughter Molly wakes from her nap to find a strange baby in her mother's arms. Fearing she is being replaced, Molly rushes to Bruce, points at Zack, cries "Baby! Baby!" and generally goes berserk.

Bruce and Pat had brought out an old infant seat which Molly outgrew months before, but the moment she sees it she climbs into it and refuses to budge, trying to convince her parents she is still a baby. Just in case we were in any doubt how a child feels when a younger sibling is born.

*

July 14, evening. Zack picks up his pacifier for the first time and puts it into his mouth. He also holds his own relief bottle with both hands. We are incredibly impressed with such precocious behavior. We needn't be, as he will not remember how to do either of these things and not even try them again for several months.

The tension between us and Karen has lessened somewhat. Everybody is on his or her best behavior, realizing we may have to live together another three-and-a-half months.

*

July 15. A card arrives from Caldor's: "Dear Customer: The portraits of your recent sitting are complete and they are beautiful as only natural living color can make them. . . ."

I am elated at the news until I realize that it is a printed card which is sent to everybody, whether their portraits are beautiful as only natural living color can make them or cross-eyed and totally out of focus.

*

July 17. We go to Caldor's to pick up our portraits. I am a trifle disappointed that the jolly photographer who called Zack "Smiley" is not the man who is at the booth.

We are shown our portraits, and, for the most part, they are, indeed, beautiful as only natural living color can make them. The fifteen wallet-sized prints are great, and so are the three 5 × 7s and the two 8 × 10s, and, yes, they are really only $8.88. There is also a wonderful 3 × 5 portrait in 3-D, framed in a tacky Ramada-Inn-type wooden frame, which costs another $8 and which I have to have.

Then the man shows us three 11 × 14s which, he admits, are a little more expensive. How much more expensive?

"Well," says the man, "with your eleven-by-fourteens, you're looking at sixty dollars—and they would run you at least three to six hundred dollars anywhere else."

We are not much tempted by the 11 × 14s. The expressions on Zack's and Suzanne's faces on these pictures could be a bit better, but mainly all three of them are out of focus. We realize that some of our favorite poses are not here, and I remark to Suzanne that the choice of which shots to blow up to 11 × 14, which to 8 × 10, and so on probably has nothing to do with the quality of the pictures themselves.

"Quite right," says the man proudly, having overheard my remark. "Your first three poses we automatically make into your wallet sizes, your 5 × 7s and your 8 × 10s. Your next three poses we make into your 11 × 14s, and your next one after that becomes your 3-D."

"And what becomes of the rest of them?" I say. "Do you throw them away?"

The man shrugs.

Well, the choice seems clear: We want everything but the 11 × 14s, and, unlike my sister, I am willing to have the man throw into the trash the out-of-focus portraits of my wife and son. I am not enamored of the frame on the 3-D portrait and I dicker with the man about removing it, but he misunderstands, and says the price would still be the same without the frame. I realize he thinks I'm trying to get a cheaper rate by taking the 3-D shot unframed, so we just give the man our $16.88 and take our pictures.

"Then you don't want your beautiful 11 × 14s?" he says sadly.

"I'm afraid not," I say, weakening briefly, then remembering they are out of focus and that we have no use for them whatsoever.

*

July 18. To supplement Suzanne's breast milk, today Zack gets his first taste of solid food. By solid food, I hasten to point out, I do not mean strip-sirloin-medium-rare-with-bernaise. Solid food in Zack's case means flakes of rice cereal mixed with formula till it is soupy, which you feed to him with a little spoon. Unlike many babies, Zack takes an instant liking to the cereal, and even manages to swallow—a learned skill. A small portion of the cereal finds its way into his mouth, but the bulk of it goes on his chin, on his cheeks, in his eyes, in his nostrils, in his hair, on his chair, and on the person feeding him.

As time passes we will mix less formula into it and make it less soupy. We will mix it with pulverized beef, chicken, fruits, and vegetables which we will process in the Cuisinart, freeze in ice cube trays, and then thaw individually for his meals.

Today is also Zack's first time in his playpen. He seems happy in it. Whenever he is happy now, he squeals. It is a joyful sound, and it is extremely hard on the ears. It is so loud, it is as if he is miked. He also squeals when he is unhappy. The unhappy squeal is, of course, even harder on the ears.

Suzanne absentmindedly calls our cat Gladys Zack: "OK, Zack, get off my desk." What could this mean?

*

July 21. I feed Zack rice cereal for the first time and manage to get a considerable amount on the environment. Zack himself is wearing his food. As I scrape the food off his chin and shovel it back into his mouth, a curious thing happens—I get a distinct sense memory of my parents scraping food off my chin as a baby and shoveling it back into my mouth.

For his next meal of the day I hear Suzanne say: "Come on, Zack, it's time for your solid food bath."

*

July 22. Another checkup at the pediatrician. Zack is overtired and cries the whole time we are in the waiting room. When we go into the office the nurse gives him his next DPT shot and he cries all the harder.

Suzanne is concerned that Zack is not getting enough milk when he breast-feeds. Eric and Carol have recently told us that Jordan weighs 16 pounds 8 ounces. Dr. Schonfeld tells us that Zack weighs 12 pounds 14 ounces, which is below the curve. We tell the doctor that Zack seems no longer willing to do the extra work of sucking the milk out of Suzanne's breasts, especially when it flows so much more easily from the bottle.

Dr. Schonfeld says that Zack is weaning himself and suggests that it is time for Suzanne to give up breast-feeding. Suzanne nods. When we leave the doctor's office, both Suzanne and Zack are in tears.

Suzanne tells me that she is desolate that she has to give up this important connection with her son. I point out that she has breast-fed him for almost five months, she did a great job, and now she will be able to have much more freedom in her life, but she is difficult to console.

By evening Zack is running a fever of 102.2 from his reaction to the DPT shot and is very cranky. I am a lot less nervous this time, and spend the evening assembling the Friedman crib, which, because it is not new, of course has no instructions. It is a sort of graduate construction project for dads.

*

July 23, morning. Zack is a little better than last night, but not well enough to go with Suzanne for her weekly day in New York. Suzanne, who has recently gotten accustomed to travelling back and forth on the Jitney with Zack in her arms, is momentarily depressed. Then she realizes she will be free to go shopping for bathing suits in the city and she perks right up.

*

July 24. Zack has been impossible for the past two days, crying continually, hardly ever sleeping. We realize we must get him on some kind of a rigid schedule, implement The Cure, and do whatever we can to stop this.

We have to find a new nanny. In the mail comes a promising resume from a prospective nanny named Callie who is only eighteen but who runs a day-care center in the Midwest and one from a girl named Jennifer who works at the Hinky-Dinky Market in Seattle. Both sound worth interviewing.

For dinner we go to a Mexican restaurant with the Friedmans, who realize to their extreme embarrassment that our waitress is a mom from their playgroup. Bruce confides he doesn't feel right being waited on by a mom from their playgroup and spends a goodly portion of the meal overcompensating for his embarrassment by joking with the waitress, apologizing for her having to wait on him, and telling her anecdotes about all the menial jobs he's ever had.

*

July 25. Suzanne's friend Laurie in Dallas has one baby and is nine months pregnant with her second. She suggests a schedule for Zack which worked for her. Suzanne gets Zack on Laurie's baby's schedule today. He appears to respond to it and begins sleeping better immediately.

We interview Callie on the phone and find her intelligent and charming and outrageously eager to work long hours. In the course of the interview she says that she is a foster child, which is one reason she wants so much to be a nanny, to be able to give little kids what she never had. Suzanne asks if she ever sees her real parents, and Callie says no, the court won't let her. Why not?

"Well," says Callie, "because my parents beat me when I was little, and my mother murdered my sister."

Ummm, yes. We try to appear unshocked by this, but what is going through both of our minds is the famous theory that abused children often become child abusers themselves. We tell her we'll call her references and get back to her.

*

July 26, morning. While sweeping the deck, Esther has shaken the tree in which Zack's Jolly Jumper hangs, in order to make any loose pine needles fall. Unbeknownst to any of us, there is a hornet's nest in this tree, and Esther's shaking causes five hornets to attack her. Esther recovers.

I peer into the huge tree and locate the hornets' nest, and the sight of it fills me with dread. It is exactly the size, shape, and color of a mummy's head. I know I will have to get rid of it to protect Zack.

*

July 26, evening. We have now called all Callie's references and they all rave about her. Suzanne and I agree that Callie sounds like a great girl, and we think it horribly ironic and cruel to punish a victim for having been victimized . . . and yet. And yet how can we hire somebody to take care of our son whom we even *think* might one day slip and do something awful to him?

We call up four psychologists and ask their opinions. They all say she might well be perfect, but we'd be fools to hire the girl. We realize we have to tell Callie no, and what's more we cannot tell her why. We are very sad.

*

July 27. I buy a can of hornet spray. Late at night I fire it repeatedly, like an automatic rifle, at the mummy's head until the entire can is empty. Hornets come spilling out of the nest, dazed, buzzing angrily, flying about, dying. I beat it back inside the house and watch them make kamikaze runs at the screen door. In an hour there is a pile of dead hornets under the mummy's head. I feel unpleasantly like I have napalmed a village in Vietnam, but I know Zack will be safe now.

*

July 28. I telephone Callie and say we have decided against her because of her age. I say the nanny we have now is twenty-four and we really do need someone older. Callie says she understands. I feel rotten.

I see hornets entering the mummy's head and I realize I have not killed them all. I go back to buy more hornet spray, and a guy at the hardware store tells me the only way to destroy a hornet's nest is to knock it out of the tree, soak it in gasoline and set it on fire. I don't look forward to such a grisly activity, but I sense he must be right.

*

July 29. Zack is nearly five months old. His new schedule is working out unbelievably well. He no longer needs to cry himself to sleep whenever he goes to bed. He no longer needs us to rock him to sleep for an hour every night. He sleeps for several hours at a stretch. Laurie's baby's schedule is going to change our lives!

*

July 31. Suzanne is trying to feed Zack his solid food with a tiny spoon. He is turning his face this way and that to avoid her, but her spoon is relentless. While she tries to feed him she is singing a little song she made up. It is roughly to the tune of "Skip to My Lou, My Darling," and it goes: "Everywhere you look, there's Mommy with a spoon/ Everywhere you look, there's Mommy with a spoon . . . ."

Zack is getting huge. His feet are now twice the size they were when he was born. Suzanne has bought a little headboard with a plastic mirror to fit inside his crib. He stares at his reflection incessantly and appears hypnotized by it.

Everytime I look at him for more than a minute I think: "God is he cute—and I am responsible for him for life."

*

August 2. In the morning I am feeding Zack his solid food, and I have to keep pulling his foot out of his mouth every time I want to insert another spoonful. Then he holds a foot in each hand and uses his feet as deflection devices.

I put him to bed for his morning nap and he accidentally picks up his pacifier and sticks it in his mouth. He seems amazed by this. He takes it out, looks at it, and puts it back in again, and I know that he has already forgotten how he did it.

In the evening my sister Naomi, her husband Lee, and their two sons, Jonny and Joel, arrive to spend a week with us. Jonny and Joel are as knocked out by Zack as are their parents. I hadn't realized little boys cared a bit about babies.

*

August 4. Laurie's sister-in-law calls from Dallas. We think she is calling to tell us Laurie had her second baby, but it is hideous news instead—Laurie has just discovered she has breast cancer and had a mastectomy days before her delivery. Both Suzanne and I are shaken.

*

August 5. Another clash with Karen, this time about Zack's schedule. Suzanne tells me she wants to fire Karen. I point out Karen has already quit.

*

August 12. Zack has been given what are called toddler biter biscuits—teething cookies—and has fallen in love with them. He gums them and rubs them all over his face. He has a bib with pictures of two cookies on it, and he frequently grabs at the pictures and cries when he discovers they aren't real cookies. Graphic representations of objects are philosophic abstractions, and apparently too complicated for a baby's mind. Still, it is a step up from when he assumed thoughts were objects:

> It seems very strange to us, but in the early stages of mental functioning, the infant cannot easily differentiate between his mental image and the picture represented by the real object. He has to learn this. He is hungry, let us say, and hunger produces automatically the mental picture of its satisfaction. An image of the breast, or the bottle, or the associated human face, arises immediately. . . . After hundreds of repetitions, the infant gradually discovers that a mental image of his meal does not lead to satisfaction. . . . A real breast, a real bottle, leads to satisfaction. Here are the first intimations of reality, the establishment of first principles.
>
> —*The Magic Years*, Selma H. Fraiberg, p. 44.

*

August 13. Late at night, wearing army battle dress, cap, and boots, I advance on the hornet's nest, empty two cans of spray into it at close range, and then try to knock it out of the tree with long-handled pool-cleaning equipment. The hornets, as before, come zooming out, dazed and fighting for their lives. I spin this way and that, spraying them, stomping them, and the deck is alive with angry buzzing insects.

The nest is so high up and so firmly entrenched in the tree that it can only be knocked off a piece at a time. It takes me two hours to knock it all to the ground, and by then I am a sweating, jumpy, nervous wreck. I don't have the energy to douse it with gasoline and set it afire, besides which I hate the concept. But Zack is now definitely safe.

*

August 14. Suzanne returns from New York, where she saw a woman with a three-week-old baby:

"I told her I have a five-month-old, which is like saying I have a child who's twenty-five. I resisted the temptation of saying I can barely remember when he was this tiny."

Suzanne models one of her pre-pregnancy bikinis for me and asks whether I think she can wear it yet. I study her dubiously.

"Well," I tell her finally, "I would say if you can't fit the bottoms of your breasts into your bra cups, you probably ought to wait a little longer."

*

August 19, morning. Zack has started trying to crawl—he raised himself on his knees and elbows and rocked back and forth, then pitched forward on his face. While in his Swyngomatic today he leaned forward and looked up for the first time, trying to figure out what the swing was hanging from.

At the pediatrician there is good news—Zack is up to 15 pounds 4 ounces and back on his proper weight curve. Dr. Schonfeld says that he has not yet developed a sense of object permanence. This is about to change.

Another change is about to occur, she says—he's about to get a sense that he is separate from us. And with that sense will come separation anxiety and ambivalence about his caretakers.

We say that he is still crying a good deal, especially during the night. What is Dr. Schonfeld's advice on that? She turns to Zack.

"Don't be such a scuzzball, sleep through the night," she tells him, chuckling, kissing his belly, and causing him to laugh uproariously.

*

August 19, afternoon. Karen, who used to have hair down to her waist, had it all cut off today—a spontaneous decision. She brought her hair home in a ponytail from the haircutter. She doesn't look too bad in short hair, surprisingly.

For some reason, since our last spat Karen has been her old self. She is once more cheerful, industrious, and pleasant to be around. Maybe it's because she knows she's leaving.

The nanny agency in Vancouver has sent us some more resumes. One applicant states she is not interested in newborns, which makes us wonder what the agency thinks Zack is. Another applicant is a 190-pound prison librarian who says the reason she wants to become a nanny is that she is beginning to feel oppressed by the "prison patrons" of the library. A third applicant weighs 200 pounds, and I read no farther—I realize I am prejudiced, but I am not comfortable hiring a woman who outweighs me by sixty pounds.

The agency calls to give us an update and says we are going to have a hard time finding someone to work for us. Why? Because you work at home, they say.

*

August 21. We interview a prospective nanny by phone who has reportedly read the material we wrote about ourselves and really loved it. We ask her what appealed to her about what she read.

"Oh, living on the East Coast would be interesting," she says, "and one baby would be less of a bother than two."

*

August 22. Zack slept eleven hours last night—from 6:20
P.M. to 5:20 A.M.! Is this the start of something big?

*

August 23. No.

*

August 24. Zack jumps up and down when he sees his Jolly
Jumper. He makes sucking noises and reaches out when he
sees his bottle. He pulls himself into an upright sitting position in his stroller by grabbing the bar in front of him. He
takes off his hat and puts it in his mouth.

*

August 25, morning. Before our very eyes, Zack conducts
an experiment in object permanence. He lies on our bed and
looks at a large landscape on the wall painted by our neighbor
Ian Hornak. He turns away from it, then turns back, then
turns away, then turns back quickly, trying to sneak up on it.
It's still there. Amazing.

The two-month-old baby has hardly roused himself from the long
night of his first weeks in this world when he is confronted with some of
the most profound problems of the race. We invite him to study the
nature of reality, to differentiate between inner and outer experience, to
discriminate self and not-self and to establish useful criteria for each of
these categories. A project of such magnitude in academic research
would require extensive laboratory equipment and personnel . . . And
there are few grown and fully accredited scientists who can equal the
infant for zeal and energy in sorting out raw data in this project. His
equipment is limited to his sensory organs, his hands, his mouth and a
primitive memory apparatus.

—*The Magic Years*, Selma H. Fraiberg, p. 42.

*

August 25, afternoon. Suzanne tells me Zack has blonde pubic hairs. I say it isn't possible. She shows me. You have to look closely, but there they are, definitely different in quality from the others—blonde pubic hairs on a five-month-old baby. Baby or no, there is no denying his sex.

Every time I give him a bath I wash his penis. It is such a strange sensation. I sometimes worry that all this penis washing won't be good for him.

*

August 25, evening. Dinner at the home of Marilyn Bethany and Ed Tivnin. The women drift to one side of the room to talk about children, the men to the other to talk about sports and politics. I hang out with the women and talk about babies until they get bored and join the men.

*

August 26. The agency has told us that a prospective nanny named Emily is trying to decide between three families, but likes ours best and is dying to talk to us. We call her up to interview her, but she doesn't know who we are. We demean ourselves trying to refresh her memory. Finally she remembers. We ask why she liked our family best. She says she doesn't recall for sure. I tell her to bone up on our material and call us back.

Suzanne asks her an essay question: How would she introduce Zack to the world?

She thinks a moment, then says, "Well, he's five-and-a-half months, so he's walking, right?"

*

August 28. Up till now Zack has not shown more than passing interest in toys. Now if you take away his ring of big plastic keys he screams till you give them back.

He loves his bath now. When I bathe him he twists and kicks and splashes and is so frisky it is all I can do to hang onto him.

Whenever I come into the room he breaks into a huge smile. If he is drinking from his bottle, he will turn his head upside down to follow my progress across the room, grinning from ear to ear.

*

August 30. This morning Suzanne finds Zack sitting up in his crib for the first time—slumped forward, but sitting up. Later in the day I watch his attempts at crawling. He has decided that rocking back and forth on his knees and elbows is not quite all you have to do. He has added putting his behind in the air, standing on his head, and falling forward. I don't think he knows he isn't crawling yet.

*

September 1, morning. Zack's development has really gone into high gear within the past two weeks. Our friend Jan Weil, who is a child psychologist, says that Zack is "hatching"—a technical term which refers to the psychological rebirth of the child. He's developing so fast now it's like the stop-motion photos you see of blooming rosebuds.

"As adults we try to realize that every moment is precious and finite," Suzanne reflects, "and once that moment passes it will never come again. But as an adult all the moments seem so alike and you have so many of them, it's very easy to let them pass without taking advantage of them. With Zack almost every moment is distinguished by learning to do some momentous thing, like sitting up or crawling, or grasping the idea of object permanence, so it's very easy to see through him the value of time and how important every moment is."

I have been planning to go to Los Angeles between September 3 and September 7 to meet with the producers of a script I've been commissioned to write. It will be the longest I've been away from Zack since he's been born and, in my mind, about the worst time to not be with him, since he is going through so many changes now. On the other hand, it will also be nice to get away for a few days and just be by myself.

∗

September 1, evening. At a large outdoor end-of-the-summer party given by Pat Birch and Bill Becker we run into an art director named Walter Bernard who tells us that the Friedman crib is actually his and he wants it back when we're through with it. He introduces us to his twelve-year-old daughter who was the first occupant of the crib which Zack now sleeps in. I feel I am meeting a famous person.

∗

September 2, afternoon. On the beach we see Charlie Moss and his wife, Susan Calhoun, and their baby, Mary. They told us some time ago they'd been planning on taking a white water trip down the Colorado River in the Grand Canyon from September 7 to 14 with a group of their friends. Today they tell us that one of the couples in the group has dropped out. They want to know if we want to take the couple's place.

We say, gosh no, Dan's going to Los Angeles on business and we have the baby and all, and we couldn't be away from him for that long, especially now. If only it were some other time.

But when we get home we start thinking maybe it would really be fun to do it, spontaneously and without a lot of planning, and there will never really be a *good* time to go and, hey, why not live in the moment for once and go for the gusto? Zack would be safe with Karen, who, even in her worst moments, was never anything but great with him, and now she is wonderful again. And a white water river trip is something I've always wanted to do.

We vacillate. First I want to do it and Suzanne doesn't, then Suzanne wants to do it and I don't. We agree we need time alone together, away from our daily routine with Zack, but this doesn't sound like the kind of quiet, romantic vacation we need. Also the trip would necessitate our taking lots of flights, many of them in small planes, to get to the river and back, and this period of time has seen more plane crashes than any other time in history. The thought of dying in a plane crash and leaving Zack an orphan is more painful than the thought of merely dying in a plane crash.

Looking for more reasons not to go, we call up Susan and get further details of the trip, but everything we hear sounds like a reason to do it. We don't know what to do. I suggest we wait till it's over and see what we did. Meanwhile, I start packing for Los Angeles.

Suzanne calls me into the kitchen to see something. Zack is in his Jolly Jumper and Suzanne is kneeling on the floor.

"Watch," she says.

Suzanne claps her hands on the floor seven times. Zack jumps in the Jolly Jumper seven times. Suzanne claps her hands on the floor seven times. Zack jumps in the Jolly Jumper seven times. I am not sure what it is I am seeing, but I know that although horses can do something of this sort, it is very good that Zack can do it too.

I return to the bedroom to continue packing my suitcase on the bed. Suzanne brings Zack in and puts him on the bed, and he tries desperately to crawl toward me. It seems to me that he is anticipating my absence, but I know this is nonsense.

*

September 3. Suzanne drives me to the East Hampton airport, where we run into Charlie Moss and Susan Calhoun, who want to know what we've decided about the river trip. We say we don't know, that we are sort of tempted to go.

Susan says if Suzanne comes with her right now she will help her pick out the backpacks and the slickers we will need for the trip, and we allow this to decide the issue—automobile salesmen call this "closing on a minor point."

So we are going on the river trip! I kiss Suzanne goodbye and get on the plane to New York.

*

September 4, morning. I have a breakfast meeting with film producer David Ladd, who has an infant a little younger than Zack. During the course of our discussion on babies Ladd says, "Of course you must have discovered that the only disposable diapers to use are Huggies?"

"Huggies?" I say. "But *Luvs* are better than *Huggies*."

"*Luvs?*" he replies, amazed. "You're joking—Huggies are *much* better than Luvs."

It is a debate we never resolve.

*

September 4, evening. I speak to Suzanne on the phone at great length about our wills. We have not had a chance to change mine to provide for Zack, and Suzanne doesn't have a will at all. By the end of the trip we will have flown on a total of twelve planes between us. Who will bring up our baby if we both die in a plane or on the river trip?

We begin an agonizing discussion in which it is eventually decided that my sister Naomi will be appointed Zack's guardian, our East Hampton house and our New York apartment will be sold to pay for Zack's upbringing and college education, and so on, and before long we are both crying at the prospect of our son growing up as an orphan.

*

September 5. We have heard about so many tragedies involving children and swimming pools we decided some time ago that Zack should take the swimming lessons which are offered to infants. Zack is almost six months old. He will have his first swimming lesson in our pool tomorrow, Suzanne tells me on the phone, and I feel awful that I won't be there to see it.

Suzanne has bought all the backpacks, slickers, and other gear we will need for the river trip, and is alternating between fear and excitement. This is what she has learned so far:

The trip will be eighty-eight miles on the Colorado River and take six days. There will be four large rowboats or dories, with four people and an oarsman in each boat. The temperature of the river is 47 degrees, and if we fall into it we have about five minutes to get out before hypothermia sets in. We will camp out in sleeping bags and have no contact with the outside world for the six days. In the event of an accident the boatmen will try to signal passing airplanes with a mirror. At the end of the trip we will hike out of the Grand Canyon with all our possessions in our backpacks, a climb of approximately ten miles. For this reason we are advised to take as little as possible with us on the trip.

The plan is for everybody to meet in Las Vegas on September 7. The group will fly by small chartered plane from Las Vegas to Hurricane, Utah, where one member of the group owns a ranch. We'll have a cookout on the ranch, and then drive to Lee's Ferry, our point of embarkation, the following morning.

Suzanne and I send separate letters to our attorneys outlining the additions to my will. The letters will not be legally binding, but they will at least let the judge know how we wanted our son to be brought up, assuming he is interested.

✳

September 6. Tomorrow Suzanne flies from East Hampton to New York, New York to Denver, and Denver to Las Vegas. I fly from Los Angeles to Las Vegas. Then we all fly from Las Vegas to Hurricane, Utah.

Another big plane crashes today, the sixth in the current series—remember when crashes ran in threes? The total deaths in recent airline tragedies is up to something like 1700 people. There are severe electrical storms now in New York and East Hampton, and more predicted for tomorrow.

Suzanne is terrified to fly, and I can't say I blame her. I tell her that if there is still an electrical storm tomorrow she must not fly—she should call me in Los Angeles early in the morning and I will abort the river trip and fly directly back to New York. But if I don't hear from her I will meet her at the Continental gate of the Las Vegas airport at 1:30 P.M.

*

September 7, morning. I have not heard from Suzanne, and so I fly to Las Vegas, put my Los Angeles luggage in storage, and start waiting at the Continental gate where Suzanne's plane is due to come in. I realize that Suzanne will have had tremendous pressure on her to not cancel any of her flights and have me abort the trip, and will probably have flown, even if there were electrical storms. The only way I will know whether she has not crashed on one of her three flights is if she actually gets off her Continental Airlines plane at 1:30.

It is 1:30. I am at the Continental gate. Her flight lands. The people start getting off. Suzanne does not seem to be among them. I jump the barrier and start making my way against the current, through the jammed jetway to the plane, my heart pounding in my ears.

Suddenly I see her. I grab her and hug her to me so hard I hear her involuntary intake of breath. She is wearing her new yellow slicker and her backpack and I know again in that moment how terribly much I love her.

She has brought me a present—a Polaroid of Zack in his new walker. He looks about two months older than when I saw him last. His smile melts the paper it is printed on.

We race to the chartered plane, which is holding its takeoff for Suzanne's arrival.

*

September 7, evening. We are having a cookout on the ranch of Jim Trees at the edge of Zion National Park, and Suzanne is telling me things about Zack.

The walker in the Polaroid was a present for his half-birthday—which is tomorrow and which we will not be present for. The walker looks a little like a white convertible with a red leather seat. So far Zack can only drive it backwards.

At his swimming lesson the instructor dunked him four times. The first time he was so surprised he didn't cry. The other three times he did. Also, the day before Suzanne left she was taking pictures of him in the bedroom and he rolled off the bed onto his face. Suzanne says he seemed OK but she was hysterical.

*

September 8, early morning. Zack's six-month birthday. At 6:00 A.M., the time we'd be giving Zack his breakfast if we were home, we get up and climb into our river clothes and into the vans which are to take us to Lee's Ferry.

In our van are the only three couples in the group who have babies: Susan Calhoun and Charlie Moss, Jean Pagliuso and Tommy Cohen, and us. The talk on the van ride runs more to babies and nannies than to white water rapids. This morning Tommy and Jean spoke to their nanny on the phone and learned that their baby, who had been "talking" for a couple of weeks now, stopped the day they left.

We arrive at Lee's Ferry. Charlie takes one look at the river and says quietly, "Before I was semi-scared. Now I'm terrified."

We are each issued a watertight black rubber bag in which we are to put the contents of our backpacks, a watertight steel ammunition case in which we are to put anything we may need during the day, and an orange life jacket.

We are briefed about toilet facilities: Urinating will be done directly in the river, and defecating in "the unit"—a plastic wastebasket with a trash can liner in it and a toilet seat on top. The poop will be sprinkled with lime and packed out of the canyon along with all the rest of our waste.

We are briefed about what to do if the boat we are in flips over, how to stay alive in the 47-degree water, and how to help right the boat. We are told that an average of one boat flip per trip is expected:

"Keep your life jacket on at all times while you are in the boat—your life jacket is your best friend. If we flip, the boatman will look out for himself first, the boat second, and you third. Take a good look at the river. It will be your home for a week."

Charlie turns to Susan: "Stick by me, honey, I'm in trouble."

*

September 8 through 13. We spend the most exciting and exhilarating week of our lives on the river. The Grand Canyon is as spectacular as in its famous portraits, although we are looking at it from the bottom up, of course. The rapids are awesome, with waves in the midst of them as high as eighteen feet, but the oarsmen are extremely skilled and we find our way through all the right openings without flipping.

More frightening than the rapids is a rock-climbing sidetrip we take one cold and cloudy morning in something called the Silver Grotto. Clad in swimsuits, we rappel up a rock wall slicked by dripping water, swim through an icy silt pond of opaque, clay-colored water, climb up another slick wall with virtually no handholds or footholds, swim through another silt pond, and so on, till we are high enough up that a misstep and a fall would result in cracked bones or worse. Those above us reach down to pull us up when we do misstep. And as chilling as is the upward climb, the downward climb is worse. But having done it is one of the great accomplishments of my life.

And being on the river as a thunderstorm buffets us with sheets of freezing rain for three hours is not my idea of comfortable fun, but we all sing camp songs at the top of our lungs and ultimately bring the boats together in the middle of the river and pass around a bottle of Myers's rum, and when the sun finally breaks through it is as fine a feeling as I've experienced.

And camping out, which I hadn't done since I was fifteen, is surprisingly easy to get used to. And we have marvelous cookouts under the absurdly starry sky, and campfires, and more Myers's rum.

And the only way you can get clean on this trip is to jump into the 47-degree water, race out, lather up, jump in again, and again race out before you freeze to death, and it sure isn't comfortable but it sure is invigorating, and it sure is fun.

And the hike out of the canyon with our twenty-pound backpacks takes eight hours, and nobody in the group thinks he is going to make it to the top, even the athletes. Suzanne and I get separated from the rest of the group and struggle painfully and exhaustedly to the rim twenty minutes after sundown when the rest of the group is calling out the rangers to look for us, but even that is terrific, especially in retrospect.

We stay at an ancient hotel called El Tovar on the rim of the canyon the night of September 13, and the water in our shower is the first water over 47 degrees we have bathed in for a week, and our bed is somewhat more comfortable than our sleeping bags, and there is ice for our drinks at dinner for the first time, and all of that is fine too.

It is hard to recall that we have a home and a baby and a life outside of the river and the canyon, but we remember to telephone East Hampton. Karen says that Zack is perfect and happy, and we are relieved, but Suzanne tells me Zack is only perfect and happy because he thinks Karen is his mother.

*

September 14 and 15. Before flying from the Grand Canyon back to Los Angeles, I buy Zack a tiny hooded sweatshirt which says The Grand Canyon on it and which has a picture of Mickey Mouse in cowboy attire.

I pick up the Los Angeles baggage which I had checked in Las Vegas and we fly back to New York, and then to East Hampton.

Karen and Zack are waiting for us at the East Hampton airport. We can see them from the window of the plane, and it is obvious even from that far away how much Zack has grown. Zack is wearing his new Nike tennis shoes and carrying a red rose. We get off the plane and hug him and fuss over him, and he actually appears to remember us. Thank God.

When we put Zack in his crib at night I see that Suzanne taped an 8 × 10 photo of herself to the end of his crib before she left—"so he wouldn't forget me," she explains.

It is so strange being home. The river is our home, not this house. And even though Zack appears to know who we are and has learned to reach out to us to be held, we are not certain who *he* is.

"I can't imagine where he came from," Suzanne confides. "He's so big and so unfamiliar, and now I'm slim again and wearing my old clothes . . . maybe we adopted him."

That night I dream Zack begins to speak in whole sentences. I excitedly write down every word he says, but Suzanne comes in and says it's no big deal. I awake at 4:00 A.M. to the sound of Zack's crying and I start to get up, remembering it is Karen's night off and I have to give him his bottle. And as I get out of bed I know I have to be extremely careful lest I step off the sand and fall into the river.

*

September 16. Jean Pagliuso and Tommy Cohen aren't

quite as lucky as we are—their baby doesn't recognize them when they get back, and refuses to smile at them all day.

My sister Naomi is glad we're back safe, although I'm not sure about my nephews. When they heard Naomi had been named Zack's guardian they were delighted: "Oh boy, you mean if they die we get Zack?"

We consult our attorney, Arthur Klein, about changing my will, and mention Zack's escalating development, which causes Arthur to reminisce about his son Willie's.

"I used to go into Willie's room while he was sleeping and leave notes on his chest," Arthur says.

"What did the notes say?"

" 'Please don't shave and go away.' "

*

September 17. Zack is exploring my face. While I feed him solid food he grabs my chin, my cheeks, my eyes, my glasses, and squeezes them. Then he grabs the spoon and sends food flying all over the room. Then he tries to put my nose into his mouth.

*

A chair . . . is an object of one dimension when viewed by a six-month-old baby propped up on the sofa. . . . It's even very likely that the child of this age confronted at various times with different perspectives of the same chair would see not one chair, but several chairs, corresponding to each perspective. It's when you start to get around under your own steam that you discover what a chair really is. . . . The ten-month-old will study this marvel with as much concentration and reverence as a tourist in the Cathedral at Chartres. Upon leaving the underside of the chair he pauses to wrestle with one of its legs, gets the feel of its roundness and its slipperiness and sinks his two front teeth into it in order to sample its flavor and texture. In a number of circle tours around the chair at various times in the days and weeks to come he discovers that the various profiles he has been meeting are the several faces of one object, the object we call a chair.

Every object in his environment must be constructed in this way until its various aspects are united into a whole. The study of a cup will occupy him for weeks, for countless mealtimes, while the function of the cup as perceived by his mother will hardly interest him at all. To drink milk from the cup will be the least absorbing activity in connection with the cup while he is conducting his research on the nature of the cup. He examines the outer surface of the cup, explores the inner surface, discovers its hollowness, bangs it on the tray for its sound effects. Rivers of milk, orange juice, and water cascade from cup to tray to kitchen floor adding joy to the experiment. His mother, engaged in unceasing labor with sponges and mops, can hardly be blamed if she does not encourage these experiments, but she is never consulted. He is an expert at dislodging the cup in her hand and seizing it for his own purposes; he is outraged at her interference with his experiments. Before he concludes these experiments he has discovered every property of a cup that can be extracted through his study and experimentation (including breakage) and then settles down to a utilitarian view of a cup which gratifies his mother. . . .

The world he discovers is a vast and intricate jigsaw puzzle, thousands of pieces scrambled together in crazy juxtaposition. Piece by piece he assembles the fragments into whole objects and the objects into groups until he emerges with a fairly coherent picture of the tiny piece of world he inhabits.

—*The Magic Years*, Selma H. Fraiberg, pp. 52–54.

✳

September 20. The nanny agency sends us material on two more nannies—a girl named Deb, who is a cosmetologist and has no nanny experience, and a girl named Rebecca, who's a graduate of a Canadian nanny school. Suzanne phones Rebecca first, but Rebecca says that she read our material and she isn't interested in us.

Suzanne is crushed and hangs up, then decides she would like to know why we are being rejected. I am mortified to hear Suzanne wants to call back and ask why Rebecca isn't interested in us—have we been reduced to crawling after nannies who reject us? Suzanne says Rebecca is the only girl we've been sent recently who's a graduate of a nanny school, and she needs to know why we are unacceptable to her.

I do not need to know. I can imagine a number of reasons why—she doesn't like people who work at home, she doesn't like writers, she doesn't like New York, she doesn't like how we look in the picture we sent—I don't want to know. Suzanne wants to know. She calls Rebecca back, and, as I cringe, asks why we are unacceptable.

"Well, let's see," says Rebecca, "you're the family with the five-year-old, right?"

We call Deb in Storm Lake, Iowa, and interview her at length. It's true she doesn't have any nanny experience, but she has done a lot of babysitting, loves children, doesn't mind long hours, and sounds like a really nice person. She has been trained as a cosmetologist, but is currently working as a seamstress in a jeans factory. When we hang up Suzanne says, "Well, if we hire her and she isn't a good nanny, at least she can mend our jeans and do my hair."

Karen has been so great of late—especially compared to most of the nannies we've been interviewing—that we are a little sad she's going. We have thought several times of asking her to stay, but we know she wouldn't, and we also sense that part of the reason she's been so good is that she knows she's leaving.

*

September 21. Zack's swimming teacher, a mother in her early thirties named Ricki, comes to give him his second lesson. Ricki takes him in the pool without his diaper, holds him against her ample breast, with his head facing her and his stomach in the water, and walks across the pool, moving his legs up and down, saying, "Kick-kick-kick-kick-kick." She holds him at her side against her waist, moving his arms, saying, "Paddle-paddle-paddle-paddle-paddle." Then she holds him against her chest again, counts, "1 . . . 2 . . . 3 . . .", blows in his face, and dunks his head in the water.

When Zack is dunked, his face takes on a betrayed expression and he bursts into tears, but the rest of us—Ricki, Karen, Suzanne, and I—clap and cheer and try to convince him in loud, enthusiastic voices that he has just done the greatest thing in the world. After a few moments Zack looks at us and starts to smile, the tears still in his eyes.

He is so influenced by our approval, so anxious to please us—just as the horoscope he was given said—he can be convinced that being dunked in the water is an acceptable way to spend one's time. He is so endearing, his smile so ingratiating, I can barely stand it.

Now it is my turn to give him lessons. I hold him against my chest and we do kick-kick-kick-kick-kick. I hold him against my waist and we do paddle-paddle-paddle-paddle-paddle. I hold him against my chest and dunk him, and the look of betrayal when I dunk him causes me almost physical pain. I hate doing this, I really hate it, and the thought that it could save his life doesn't make it much easier.

Ricki has brought along her 13-month-old son, Victor. She tells us that a couple of weeks ago, Victor fell in her pool when she was in the house and he was able to swim to the edge of the pool and save his own life. She has Victor demonstrate how he saves his own life. I wish that I were more impressed by the demonstration. Victor looks like he is on the verge of drowning. Victor begins to cry, and Ricki claps and cheers and tries to convince him and the rest of us how well he did and how much he loves swimming.

After Zack's lesson is over, Ricki takes Victor into our kitchen and changes him on our kitchen counter. When he is lying on the counter nude, she points to his penis and asks Karen what she makes of all those red welts. Karen doesn't know, but I am not thrilled that little Victor has come here with red welts all over his penis and exposed Zack to whatever it is he has.

*

September 22, evening. Suzanne calls me into Zack's room and tells me to watch. Zack is in his crib, staring through the bars. Suzanne dips down below his field of vision and bobs back into view again, shouting, "Peekaboo!" Zack thinks it's about the funniest thing anybody ever said to him, and laughs uproariously.

She does it again and again, then excitedly explains to me that playing peekaboo is a very advanced thing for him to do, because it presupposes object permanence—when Suzanne ducks down out of sight, Zack has begun to realize that she continues to exist, he just can't see her. Suzanne calls up our child psychologist friend, Jan, and tells her that Zack has learned to play peekaboo. Jan is very impressed.

On the news tonight is a story about a tropical storm in the South Atlantic whose winds are estimated as high as 150 miles per hour. There is speculation that the storm could come ashore along the Carolina coast, in which case it could cause tremendous damage. Unless the storm blows itself out, it could hit in five days. Fortunately, we are too far north for it to pose a threat to us.

*

September 23, morning. Zack is nearly seven months old. Dr. Schonfeld tells us Zack has gained two pounds—he now weighs 17 pounds 4 ounces. Dr. Schonfeld is delighted Zack can play peekaboo and speaks of its significance in terms of object permanence and self versus non-self. Then she kisses him on the belly, Zack chortles, and the nurse gives him his third DPT shot—betrayed again.

*

September 23, evening. Suzanne is talking to her father on the phone, bragging about Zack's ability to play peekaboo. Her father listens patiently for a few minutes as she explains the significance of peekaboo in terms of self versus non-self and object permanence, then, chuckling skeptically, he says, "Suzanne, you're gonna think yourself to *death*."

The tropical storm in the Atlantic Ocean has become Hurricane Gloria and is moving steadily toward the Carolinas. Dr. Neil Frank at the National Hurricane Center in Miami—a Robert Cummings look-alike—is beginning to warn television viewers that Gloria may be one of the worst storms of the century. People in the Carolinas have been put on a hurricane watch, and many are boarding up their houses and getting out. I am glad that we don't live on the Carolina coast.

*

September 24, afternoon. Suzanne says to me today, "I just did something I never thought I'd do."

"What's that?" I say.

"Well, Zack was gumming a teething cookie and it was getting all mushy. Then it broke into a couple of pieces, so I grabbed it and ate it."

"Why did you do that?"

"I was afraid he'd choke on it."

"Why didn't you just throw it away?"

Suzanne looks at me and frowns.

"Because it was a good cookie. I happen to like arrowroot cookies."

*

September 24, evening. Zack is refusing to eat his solid food. I ask what food it is and am told it's a mixture of bananas, peas, and chicken. I make a face and say I don't blame him. Suzanne says it's good, and I should eat some to show him I like it. I say she's got to be kidding. She claims it's important that Zack see I like it. I sigh and let her put a spoonful of the bananas, peas, and chicken into my mouth. I almost gag on it, but I pretend it's one of the most delicious things I've ever eaten. Zack still won't touch it.

The hurricane watch on the Carolina coast has become a hurricane warning, and more people near the shore are being evacuated. There is now talk that Hurricane Gloria could come north, possibly as far as New York and Long Island, and although they are saying this is not likely, the descriptions of the hurricane and the film clips of hurricanes in the past are starting to make us nervous. Gloria is now estimated to hit Cape Hatteras on Friday, September 27.

*

September 25. We call four references that Deb the cosmetologist has given us, and they all rave about her. We have pretty much decided to hire her, but call Deb and emphasize that it's a difficult job—she should think hard about it before deciding to accept it.

The reports about Hurricane Gloria get worse and worse. Predictions are that ten inches of rain and a tidal wave sixteen to eighteen feet high will accompany the storm. Some newsmen say Gloria will pack the force of five hydrogen bombs.

The hurricane is all anybody on TV seems to be talking about. Dr. Neil Frank of the National Hurricane Center is on camera every time we look. Dr. Frank is urging people near the shore to evacuate, repeating that Gloria is thought to be one of the most powerful and destructive hurricanes of the century, and saying uplifting things like, "We are staring down the barrel of a gun."

*

September 26. Residents of low-lying areas near the ocean are being urged by roving sound trucks in East Hampton to evacuate their homes. Those who resist are asked for the names and addresses of their next-of-kin. At 3:00 P.M. Governor Cuomo declares a state of emergency, mobilizes

600 National Guardsmen, dispatches them to Long Island, and goes on radio and TV to urge people near the shore to evacuate.

"This is not a Japanese horror movie or a movie on TV," says the governor over and over again, "This is *real*."

Suzanne and I are about a four-minute drive from the beach. How many miles is this? I get into the car, drive to the beach and watch the odometer on the way back. We are two miles from the water. Would a tidal wave come two miles inland? I doubt it, but then I don't know anything about tidal waves. We might decide it would be exciting to stay and ride out the storm if we didn't have a baby, but we *do* have a baby, and we must protect him.

We consider evacuating East Hampton and going to New York. But would New York be any better? Newscasters in New York are urging people to stock up on candles, flashlights, batteries, non-perishable foods, and to fill their bathtubs with water. In our East Hampton home we have candles, flashlights, batteries, and food, and we also have a gasoline-powered generator which is sufficient to run our refrigerator, our water pump, and a couple of lights if—no, *when*—the power fails. In our New York apartment we don't have any food, perishable or otherwise, and if the power there fails we have no recourse.

Since they still don't really expect the hurricane to swing north and reach Long Island, we elect to stay in East Hampton and gamble that Gloria will come ashore at Cape Hatteras and run out of steam. We buy several extra cans of gasoline for the generator. We hold a practice drill with the generator to see that it is working properly and to figure out which lights it runs.

We had told Deb she should call us today to let us know if she really wants to come to work for us. Deb calls and says she wants the job. We tell her she's hired. She will come to New York on October 26.

They are saying on TV that tomorrow morning we will know for sure whether Long Island is in danger. We take in all our outdoor furniture and hoses and floodlights and potted plants and go to sleep, setting the alarm for 6:30 A.M. so there will still be time to take emergency measures if necessary, although what those might be I'm not quite sure.

*

September 27. Hurricane Day. By 6:30 A.M. the worst scenario has materialized: According to the reports on TV, Gloria has not made landfall on Cape Hatteras as expected, has headed straight north, and is now expected to come ashore somewhere on Long Island.

We deeply regret that we didn't go to New York last night after all. There is nowhere to go now. I feel extremely guilty that we have needlessly jeopardized Zack's safety by remaining here in the path of the storm.

We race around the house, taping windows, then realize this is not enough. We decide I should go to the lumberyard and get plywood to nail over as many windows as possible before the hurricane hits.

At 7:45 A.M. I drive the Jeep to the lumberyard, and the scene there is reminiscent of Japanese horror movies before the arrival of the monsters. People are racing around, frenziedly buying up the last sheets of plywood. Lumberyard workers are no longer willing to cut wood to size or to be polite, because they're rushing to close up and go home. I buy six sheets of four-by-eight-foot CDX plywood, tie them to the roof of the Jeep and head home. The wind is already pretty strong, the sky has gotten dark and it has started to rain.

With Suzanne's and Karen's help I nail all six sheets of plywood over most of the big plate glass windows in the kitchen and master bedroom, deftly shattering one of the windows in the process, but by 10:00 A.M. we are as ready as we will ever be.

The only room in our house that doesn't have windows to the outside is the master bathroom. We squeeze Zack's playpen and a supply of flashlights, batteries, and candles into the bathroom, and Suzanne needlessly tapes the glass shower doors. When I tease her about this, she replies testily that she is not willing to risk having a tree crash through the bathroom wall, shatter the shower doors and send shards of glass flying into Zack's eyes to blind him, for God's sake.

In addition to the hurricane warnings there are now tornado warnings. Suzanne had experience with tornados as a little girl in Kansas, before she moved to Texas. If the radio reports a tornado heading our way we plan to go into the cellar and cower. Otherwise we arc better off in the bathroom.

The wind begins playing havoc with the trees which surround our house. Zack plays with his toys, oblivious to the hysteria on all sides of him, and crawls his first three steps.

Suzanne and I assemble an inflatable walker called a Funaround which we just bought for him—four inner-tube-like rings stacked with the smaller ones on top, and wheels on the bottom. Zack sits in the middle of the tubes, looking like the Michelin Man, and propels himself around the floor with great gusto, runs over Wendell's tail and traps Gladys against the wall, reaching out to pat her head and ears. Gladys, who is barely civil to anyone but me and Suzanne, allows this without biting or hissing or scratching, and I am deeply grateful for her indulgence.

Looking for busywork to calm my pre-hurricane jitters, I replace old baby pictures of Zack in my wallet with new ones, marvelling at how the old ones don't even look like him anymore.

Just before 11:00 A.M. our power fails. I wait till 12:00 and then go outside to start the generator. It is a bit difficult walking against the wind, but exciting to be outside. The wind is frightening in its intensity, the trees bend low to the ground and we hear limbs start to snap off, but nothing worse happens.

By 3:30 P.M. word comes over the radio that Hurricane Gloria has made landfall at Jones Beach and the worst is suddenly over. We have survived the crisis. We are safe and our baby is safe. We are immensely relieved. We have a tremendous sense of anticlimax.

We drive to the beach and look at the highest surf I have ever seen—the waves are positively boiling. We are amazed to behold what is and is not damaged. The houses on the dunes have not been touched, but farther inland there is a lot of damage—the largest trees in town, many sixty and seventy feet high, have crashed to the ground, missing houses and churches by inches. Several houses have lost their roofs, another has burned to the ground. There do not appear to be any deaths in our area.

We go home and start cleaning up. By dark we have filled thirty large garbage bags with leaves. We have been told we'll probably be without electricity for about a week, so we use the generator selectively, conserving our gasoline, using candles in rooms where there is no electricity, turning off the generator for the night.

＊

October 5. Our electricity finally came back on last night, after a week. It has been an interesting week: On TV there was a report that a chemical called DEHP, which is present in all soft vinyl products like baby bottle nipples and pacifiers, causes liver cancer.

Zack will be seven months old in three days. He has learned to roll into my mini-office in the kitchen and take the keys out of my filing cabinet and take the papers off my desk and put them into his mouth. He has also learned how to stand up in his crib, how to blow a little train whistle we bought him, how to dip a plastic cup into his bathwater and drink from it or to drink from his bathwater directly, how to reach out for Suzanne and make a noise that sounds like "Mum-mum." And I find that when I hold him in my arms and bury my nose in his hair I am overcome with such feelings of love that I cannot stop kissing him.

Tonight Suzanne and I go to our local restaurant, the Laundry, and she tells me she saw a woman in overalls who was about seven months pregnant.

"I got very nostalgic for when I was pregnant. Every time I see a pregnant woman now I want to go up to her and tell her what a treat she has in store for her."

"You mean you no longer want to laugh viciously and tell her how terrible it's going to be?"

"No, because it isn't terrible anymore. Either that or I'm getting used to it."

Billy Bonbrest, the manager of the restaurant, comes over to our table and asks us how long we've been together. We say nine years and inquire why he is asking.

"Every time I see you, you always seem so happy together and so interested in each other," he says. "I only know two other couples who seem as happy as you do, and they live in Europe—it gives an old bachelor hope."

When our friends first learned we were pregnant they warned us how much a baby would change our lives. I'd say that this has happened. I'm a guy who has an infant seat in his Porsche, diapers in his glove compartment, and a pot of nipples and pacifiers always boiling on his stove. I'm a guy who gets up at 3:00 A.M. to give his son a late bottle, which is about the time I used to go to bed.

I might have had a sex change operation and become a nun, but outside of that I do not think my life could possibly have changed more than it did by becoming a father. And when my little son looks up at me and breaks into his wonderful toothless smile, my eyes fill up and I know that having him is the best thing I will ever do.

If you have children of your own, I hope some of the things we went through with Zack sounded familiar to you. If you don't have children and are considering it, I hope I have given you enough information to make a decision one way or another.

And finally, Zack, I hope that when you are old enough to read this yourself, you will learn how much we loved you, even when you were too young to understand. Who knows— maybe some day you'll write a book about *me*.

*